uni
LIFEHACKS

uni
LIFEHACKS

INCLUDING INSIGHTS FROM SOME OF THE UK'S MOST SUCCESSFUL STUDENTS

GEORGE MACGILL WITH DAVID JACOB

A portion of all author royalties will be donated to StudentMinds, "the UK's student mental health charity." They 'empower students and members of the university community to look after their own mental health, support others and create change'.

CONTENTS

INTRODUCTION

Uni life. It's a unique purgatory between being a young person and an adult. As a young person, your responsibilities are minimal; you probably don't have a mortgage, work a 9-5 job or look after any children. However, you've also got all the freedom of an adult: you can do whatever you want, whenever you want. You can decide on your own schedule and pursue any goals that you may have. It's a time of immense change and opportunity, which if used wisely, can be some of the best years of your life. However, this change and opportunity is a double-edged sword. The lack of good advice or a strong support system can result in disastrous consequences for uni students every single year.

I experienced both sides of that double-edged sword at uni. On the one hand, I met some of my closest friends; I experienced some of my most treasured memories and became the person I am today, while on the other, I made plenty of mistakes before getting to that point and came incredibly close to dropping out. Like a lot of students, I was told that university was going to be a time I would remember for the rest of my life, and some said I would even 'find myself'. After a year, the only things I remembered were being painfully hungover and being behind on my degree. And the only thing I really found out about myself was how deep I could enter my overdraft.

I was miserable. I was bored of my degree, my health was dreadful, and my finances may as well have resembled the worst day of the 2008 recession. I felt that society had sold me a dream about university and I had been completely duped. There was a point in my second year where I felt lost, and I had decided I was going to drop out. (If this were the X-Factor, this would be the part where the Coldplay music kicks in).

Driving home on a freezing December night right at the end of the term, it felt like nothing was going my way at uni. I had blown my entire student loan, lost my phone the night before, and I hadn't eaten in over 24 hours. All I wanted to do was get home, eat something and start figuring out how I was going to tell friends and family that I had decided to drop out. As I drove, I began to gradually realise that I had massively underestimated the amount of petrol I needed for the journey home… I suddenly found myself trapped on the side of a motorway with an empty petrol tank at 1 AM. To make matters worse, I had no money, no phone to contact anyone, there wasn't a car in sight, and it was blisteringly cold outside. I faced sleeping in my car on the side of the motorway until I could get help in the morning.

Fortunately for me, the story didn't end that way. In a miraculous turn-of-events, an off-shift AA van happened to drive past my car and spot me. He saw me; a shell of a human being, and decided to take pity on me, even filling up my petrol tank free of charge (without me even asking!) I pleaded to take his bank details, but he refused. On that drive back, I had never felt so lucky in my entire life. Reflecting on the situation the next day, I realised two things:

1. **I was the cause of all my problems** – There was a common denominator in all the problems that had occurred so far at university – *me*. *I* had blown my entire student loan. *I* had lost my phone. *I* had messed up my health (nobody else shoved vodka or junk food down my throat). *I* had sat around waiting for my degree to fulfil me, instead of going out and actually doing

anything. *I* had tried to put the blame on every other possible factor other than myself; my university, my degree, my social group, and even society in general at one point. Unfortunately for my ego, the blame was completely on me.

2. **I had unlimited freedom and opportunities** – I had some lectures and seminars that I had to attend (or at least keep up a moderate attendance rate.) I also had some exams and essays every term that I had to do. Apart from that, I was completely free to do whatever I wanted whenever I wanted. I realised I had a rare period of my life where I had absolutely no *real* responsibilities. I could experiment and make mistakes without any real consequences. If I wanted to watch a Game of Thrones marathon, I could. Or, if I wanted to run an actual marathon, I could do that too. I would never get another time in my life with so much freedom and opportunity.

After realising this, the rest of my time at university was nothing short of brilliant. I got the best grades I had ever received (despite studying less than I was doing before), my physical and mental health was considerably better, I never went into my overdraft again, and my social life was more active than it was during the first term of Freshers!

Now, looking back at my overall time at uni, it was a true roller coaster journey. I left not just with a degree but some moments that I will hold fondly forever. During my time at university, I set up and ran two student businesses. The first was a juice business, which went on to be the first student company in the UK to get stocked at an on-campus supermarket, and the second was a Hot Tub rental business, that expanded to nine cities in just six months. I also beat hundreds of competitors across the UK to be in the Adidas advert for the FIFA World Cup. There were also some definite lows (aside from the motorway incident) on that roller coaster journey. To name just a few:

- 🕊 Arriving as a Fresher not knowing how to cook and having my new flatmate teach me how to boil pasta.

- 🕊 Putting a hot tub inside our student house living room for a Halloween house party. Only to then receive a text from our landlord saying he was ten minutes away and was about to do a surprise inspection!

- 🕊 Finding out my first attempt at a student business was less legal than I first thought. (It turns out you can't run a food business out of a student kitchen where your housemates had their pre-drinks the night before.)

- 🕊 Having to attend a last minute disciplinary meeting with my university just before the start of a night out. The theme of the night out was cabaret, so I had to attempt to have a serious conversation in the meeting with a full face of makeup and rocking the tightest outfit you have ever seen.

- 🕊 Having to miss my graduation as I was called up for jury service, during which I never even saw a case!

Why We Wrote This Book

After looking at some of the mistakes I made while at university, my only regret was not finding solutions for them earlier.

The first problem was – I didn't have a time machine to go back and speak to my younger self. However, I realised that there were still thousands of university students across the UK who still had time on their side. There are plenty of guides on how to choose your university, but there wasn't a guide on how to *actually* make the most out of it... So, I decided to turn what I had learnt into a book.

The second problem was – I was a terrible writer. However, my friend Dave is a great writer. He's currently at uni, thus was able to offer a current student's perspective. He was fortunate (or unfortunate) enough to make similar mistakes, but during his A-Levels. The difference, however, was that he used his gap year to learn how to avoid falling into the mistakes that I stumbled into, meaning that by his first year at uni, he was in a far better position than I was.

One of the first things we agreed on was that most advice given to us before we came to university was utterly useless. We're sure you've heard some of these too. Here are some examples and how we often felt like responding:

🖐 *Pointless Piece Of Advice #1* – "Balance your time between your studies and having fun."

The Reality – "I have two essay deadlines next week, I have a sports match tonight, it's my best friend's birthday party this weekend, I've not called home in ages, and I've got a date tomorrow. **How** do I actually organise all of this and not just exist in a constant state of being overwhelmed?"

🖐 *Pointless Piece Of Advice #2* – "Who you live with and where you live is so important at university, it literally shapes your entire time there! Make sure you make the right choice about your housing and housemates!"

The Reality – "I have three different groups of friends looking to live with me, and I barely know the city or where the best place to live is… **How** do I make the correct decision?"

🖐 *Pointless Piece Of Advice #3* – "Make sure you don't spend all your money before the end of the term or max out your overdraft!"

The Reality – "I've just had to pay rent and heating bills this week. Now I've got to do my weekly shop, which costs a fortune, my sports team wants me to pay £90 in membership fees, and

I am going out tonight which costs me £30 on a cheap night… **How** am I supposed to not live like a monk and stay out of my overdraft?"

🖐 *Pointless Piece Of Advice #4* – "When you are applying for graduate jobs, make sure you write a good CV and just be confident in the interview room!"

The Reality – "I've sent off loads of CV's, and I haven't had a single response. Secondly, in the few interviews I've had, I choked when asked a question and my mind went blank! **How** do I just 'be confident' when any mistake I make could result in me missing out on my dream job?"

🖐 *Pointless Piece Of Advice #5* – "Don't get too stressed about it all – just relax!"

The Reality – "I have three exams next week, I am struggling to sleep and now the person I have been in a relationship with for a year has decided to break up with me. On top of all that, the summer internship I applied for has just rejected me too… **How** do I 'just relax'?!"

🖐 *Pointless Piece Of Advice #6* – "Uni is one of the most social periods of your life. Go out and meet as many people as you possibly can."

The Reality – "Really? I wasn't sat in my room with nerves because I just forgot to be a 'social butterfly'… **How** do I stop the sickening feeling in my stomach, constantly saying 'err' and worrying about making the wrong impression?"

Ultimately, what you want to get out of university is your choice. You may want to get a first-class degree or simply scrape by and get a 2:1. You may want to start your own night out, blog, or excel at the sport you play. This book isn't here to tell you what to do, it aims to aid you in achieving whatever it is that you want. It doesn't matter if you are a third year in your last term or a fresher just about to start uni, you will find value in this book.

An issue with writing a book about university is that there are so many universities, hundreds of subjects, and even more students, with a whole host of different perspectives and aspirations. With that in mind, we decided to sit down with over 50 of the UK's most successful students to find out what their secret was. They have been featured in BBC News, The Times, The Guardian, The Huffington Post, The Metro, The Tab, The Independent, Business Insider, Buzzfeed and Forbes to name just a few. They come from a variety of different backgrounds, they all lead different lives, and all have a different story to tell, showing how much it is possible to achieve just as a student.

How To Read This Book

This book isn't supposed to be read like a novel. There's no traditional structure to it, we just wanted to cut the fat and give you the most usable advice that you can actually apply. A lot of authors stretch what could be a twenty-page essay into a whole book. We wanted to do the opposite, and turn what could be twenty books into just one book. We looked to cover every area of uni life and focus on the key 20% which will bring you 80% of the results.

Feel free to read this book from start to finish or as it relates to your life. If you're a Fresher looking to enjoy yourself, you don't have to force yourself through reading *Goodbye Procrastination; Hello Productivity* right now if you don't want to. You can come back to it when your academic commitments start to pick up. Instead, feel free to skip to Chapter 1 – Goodbye Procrastination; Hello Productivity. If you're a third year who is looking to take things seriously, sit down and get stuck into *Goodbye Procrastination; Hello Productivity,* or Chapter 6 – *Be The 1% Of The Graduate Job Market.*

Before you begin reading, have a skim over the world's longest contents page and pick the parts that catch your eye. Leave the book on your desk and come back to it whenever you have a problem. If your student loan dries up midway through the semester, and you're trying to find ways to cut your budget, check out Chapter Five – *Staying Out Of Your Overdraft*. Want to kick start a fitness regime after Christmas? Read Chapter Seven – *The Uni Student Health & Fitness Guide*. If you feel like you would like to do something different at university (e.g. start a blog, run a marathon, raise money for charity or set up a business), then read the *Creatives, Athletes, Campaigners* or *Entrepreneurs* chapters accordingly. Or, maybe you're just going through a difficult time and looking to hear a story of a student who battled adversity and came out the other side. If so, skim the Insights contents and pick the ones you feel drawn to each time you pick up the book. (However, the Insights chapter names are only there to add structure to the book. Most of them could have appeared in more than one chapter, and some of them could have been in all four chapters! We aimed to keep the Insights section as true to their original style as we could; we didn't want to remove the amazing characters from their stories, so they will all have a different feel to them. All of the Insights will have something different to add, and you may find yourself learning new things from people you wouldn't have expected to.)

As best-selling author, Tim Ferris, said in his book *Tools Of Titans*:

> "This book should be fun to read, and it's a buffet to choose from. Don't suffer through anything. If you hate shrimp, don't eat the goddamn shrimp."

We hope that you discover something in this book that you will find genuinely useful; we learnt a lot from writing it, so hopefully, you will learn as much from reading it.

PART ONE

STUDENT LIFE

This book starts, as the saying goes, at the very beginning: what is life like as a student? What does it mean to be a student? I bet if you asked one hundred students, you would get one hundred different answers.

One student may say that 'student life' means years of studying to get your degree, handing in essays and sitting in exam halls. And they'd be right. The first and foremost aim of being a student is to get a degree. Hence, the first chapter is entitled *Goodbye Procrastination; Hello Productivity*. Your degree is, of course, the reason for your time at university, and if you don't pass, well you've had yourself some costly gap years!

The first chapter looks at strategies and tactics you can use to be as productive and organised as possible during your time at university, so you can get the best return on the time you invest in your work. Whether you are looking to work hard to get a first-class degree, or simply enjoy university and do as little work as possible, this chapter will be of use to you.

Another student might say that 'student life' means living in squalid conditions with constant drama occurring between hungover, hormonal, or homesick students. And they'd be right too. Before university, you lived with your family who looked after you, and your friends from school and college were usually part of the same geographic and socio-economic background as you. Now at university, you are all of a sudden living away from home, often in substandard conditions, while having to navigate your way through all of the flatmate politics with people from a variety of backgrounds. The second chapter is *Housing & Housemates: Heaven or Hell*. It offers guidance on choosing whom to live with and where, as well as ways you can hack some of the least popular student activities such as cleaning, laundry and ironing.

Finally, another student might say that 'student life' means trying to cook and get by on a budget that is getting smaller and smaller by the day. And they wouldn't be wrong. Long gone are the days of those home-cooked meals, you now have to cook your own meals (or blow all your student loan on eating out faster than you can say Wagamama).

The third and final chapter in the student life section is *The Student Chef's Cheat Sheet*. During this chapter, we sit down with the viral phenomenon *Mob Kitchen* to get some of their best student recipes, as well as explore all the best Uni Lifehacks for your student kitchen, from a sure-fire system to avoid washing up arguments with your flatmates to seven game-changing items that most student chefs don't have.

Ready? *Let's Begin.*

Goodbye Procrastination; Hello Productivity

"Tomorrow is often the busiest day of the week."

—SPANISH PROVERB

"One of these days I'm going to get
help for my procrastination problem."

—UNKNOWN

How To Conquer Procrastination

Where better to start than procrastination? It's the ultimate student kryptonite. That invisible feeling of resistance which prevents students from doing the things they know they should be doing. Imagine if there was a switch you could flick right now that stopped you from procrastinating ever again. From that point on you'd never waste a single moment putting off what you know you should be doing. Imagine how different your life would look in the space of one week? One month? One year? It would be astonishing.

Not all tasks are created equally in the mind of a procrastinator. Procrastination only arises when faced with a difficult or daunting task. For example, nobody ever puts off binging on Netflix or scrolling through Instagram, they're easy to start. However, when you have an exam or a presentation on the horizon, that's when you feel the urge to delay; often with the aforementioned Netflix and Instagram! Procrastination is often caused by a feeling of being overwhelmed, the thought of writing a 3,000-word essay or a fifteen-page lab report sounds terrifying, so you keep putting it off. *"It's fine, I'll start it tomorrow"* you tell yourself. Before you know it, it's the day before the deadline, and you hate yourself for not starting earlier.

The best way to conquer procrastination is breaking the task you are putting off into small manageable chunks that are easy to start. One of the most effective ways to do this is the Pomodoro Technique, where you work for twenty-five minutes and then take a five-minute break. For example, if you are putting off your dissertation research, tell yourself that you are going to do twenty-five minutes of reading and then you are going to take a five-minute break. Doing this takes something daunting like starting your dissertation and turns it into something achievable. Anyone can work for twenty-five minutes, especially if they have a break afterwards. The most powerful aspect of the Pomodoro technique is that it gets you over the biggest hurdle of them all… starting the damn thing! Often, after telling my-procrastinating-self that I will *"just work for twenty-five minutes"* when the twenty-five minutes was up, I had gotten so deep into the work that I continued to plough through the task for another hour without even realising it. The technique also helped me to focus and not give into distractions while studying because I knew a break was on the horizon, where I could check my phone or grab something to eat. Without that scheduled break, 'checking my phone for a minute' when I should've been working would often lead me down a procrastination 'rabbit hole'. I once found myself an hour later googling "*why is Google called Google?*"[1]

How To Apply This At University – The Pomodoro Technique

1. **Have ONE task in mind that you want to work on** – Pick the most important one!

2. **Set your timer for 25 minutes. Do NOTHING but work for that 25 minutes** – Put your phone on 'Airplane Mode' or switch it off. If any distractions come up, write them down on a to-do list and get back to your work.

3. **Take a 5-minute break at the END of the 25 minutes** – Do whatever you want for these 5 minutes. Check your phone, check social media, text your friends, or get something to eat. It's 5 minutes of freedom.

4. **Put your 25-minute timer ON again[2]** – After your break, return and do another 25 minutes of focused work. Pick the same task that you were working on if you have not completed it yet or move on to another one.

5. **Take a REAL break** – After 4-6 Pomodoro sessions try and take time off from your work for at least an hour. You will be able to relax knowing that you have spent 100 – 150 minutes completely focused on the task you were procrastinating on.

---

[1] It was actually all to do with a spelling mistake. It was supposed to be named after the mathematical term 'Googol', but the founders accidentally misspelt it. Before being called Google, it was originally called 'Backrub'.

[2] There are numerous free apps and plugins to use such as Focus Keeper, Clear Focus and Strict Workflow.

9 Apps That Will Help Make Your Degree So Much Easier

Surprisingly, it is often the small things that make the difference in the attainment of a First or a 2:1. So, stack the odds in your favour by using every little bit of help you can get. It could ultimately result in you feeling ecstatic or crushed when you get your final grades back. Here are some free apps and plugins that'll hopefully make your degree a little easier to manage:

1. **Dayboard** – Tell Dayboard the five most important things you need to do that day. Whenever you open up a new tab, it will give you a reminder of those five things right before you're about to procrastinate. If you cross off each task as you complete them, it means that you can surf guilt free and be reminded of your accomplishments when you have completed your tasks for the day. It also features a useful website blocking system, where you can block any of your Achilles' heel websites until you're ready to stop working.

    Available on: Chrome

2. **OneTab** – When doing research and you have lots of tabs open, press the OneTab button and it will collapse all your open tabs into just a single tab. You will then have a clear and concise list of web pages that you can navigate through. Using OneTab can save up to 95% of your computer's memory and prevent the fatal internet crash midway through your work!

    Available on: Chrome, Firefox, Safari (Extensions)

3. **Note Board** – This gives you the ability to make digital sticky notes that are backed up on the cloud. You can use text, images, screenshots and set notifications to remind you about specific notes.

    Available on: Chrome, Firefox

4. **Cite This For Me (CTFM)** – There's no worse feeling than staying up late all night finishing your essay only to realise you still have to do the bibliography! CTFM enables you to automatically create a bibliography. By searching the web address, ISBN or author of paper, journal or study, CTFM does the hard work for you, referencing the piece of literature in your chosen style automatically. It features a range of different referencing styles too, including Harvard, APA and OSCOLA. (An alternative app is EasyBib)

    Available on: App Store, Google Play, Chrome, *citethisforme.com*

5. **Tiny Cards** – Make your flashcards digital. Create your own flashcards as well as access thousands of other flashcards that are stored on their system on a range of topics, from Medicine to Astrology.

    Available on: App Store, Google Play

6. **Facebook News Feed Eradicator** – How many times have you found yourself mindlessly scrolling through your Facebook news feed when you've actually got important stuff to do? Facebook News Feed Eradicator does what it says on the tin – it completely eradicates your Facebook news feed so you only get messages or notifications.

    Studies have also shown that excessive Facebook use is associated with increased feelings of jealousy, low self-esteem and depression (1). Instead of seeing another photo of your aunt's cat or reading a political status that makes your blood boil, it replaces it all with a cheesy motivational quote to remind you to get things done.

    Available on: Chrome, Safari

7. **MyStudyLife** – It's easy to forget things at uni, and the online timetable that your university provides is often outdated and uneditable. MyStudyLife gives week and day timetables, it keeps track of all your lectures, seminars and exams in the cloud and sends push notifications to remind you in advance. It also enables you to colour code the calendar making it easier for you to organise and group different tasks.

    Available on: App Store, Google Play, Windows Phone, *www.mystudylife.com*

8. **Grammarly** – Never get marked down on your writing skills again. Grammarly is 'the world's leading automated proofreader'.[3] It checks '250 types of spelling, grammar, and punctuation errors, enhances vocabulary usage and suggests citations'. Even if you view yourself as a good writer, when you are up late in the library finishing that essay, it's very easy for typos to slip through without your sleep-deprived eyes picking up on them. Plus, it's useful for other non-essay related tasks too, like writing a CV or sending off an email to your tutor.

    Available on: Chrome. Safari, Firefox, Windows, Mac

9. **Asana** – University group work can get as political as a season finale of *House of Cards*. Asana is the ultimate project management tool; you can create projects, delegate tasks to specific members, and enforce deadlines. There's also a group chat function so you can talk to your team as well as a calendar where you can schedule your meetings. Asana can make the difference between you going for drinks with your group to celebrate after you finished, or passive-aggressively leaving the Whatsapp group and vowing to never speak to them again.

    Available on: App Store, Google Play

---

[3] A premium version is also available.

A Revision Habit That Will Drastically Increase The Amount Of Information You Retain

We take it you've heard of 'Mind Mapping' before? The guy who helped bring that into mainstream use, *Tony Buzan*, also has another genius revision habit that you may not be aware of. It's based on two human cognitive biases that the world's best marketers use all the time, and you probably succumb to them regularly without even knowing it.

Before we explain them, let's first do an experiment. Look at the list of names below for thirty seconds; try to remember as many as you can, then close the book and do your best to reel them off:

Tim. Jess. Gary. Nicky. Mike. Sarah. David. Sam.
Charlotte. Peter. Helen. Edward. Alice. Ryan.

Which names did you remember? The names nearer the beginning? The names nearer the end?

The average person is much more likely to remember 'Tim', 'Jess' and 'Gary' and 'Edward', 'Alice' and 'Ryan' than any other name on this list.

A. **The Primacy Effect** – It's easy to remember the beginning because it's the first thing that you saw. (E.g. why people say a first impression is so important.)

B. **The Recency Effect** – It's easy to remember the end because it's still fresh in your mind. (E.g. why stand-up comedians save their best material until the end of their show.)

The issue here is that it's a struggle to remember the middle. With that in mind, if your revision session is an hour long, you are likely to remember the first and last ten minutes far better than the middle forty minutes. With that forty minutes being two-thirds of your revision session, it makes sense to do something about it. Structure your sessions so they take into consideration the primacy and recency effects.

How To Apply This At University – The Primacy And Recency Biases

1. **Take advantage of the PRIMACY Effect** – At the start of every revision session, spend the first 5-10 minutes of it going over everything from the last session you did.

2. **Take advantage of the RECENCY Effect** – At the end of every revision session, spend the last 5-10 minutes recapping everything that you learnt in the revision session you have just completed.

How To Understand Any Degree Topic Using A Nobel Prize Winning Physicist's Technique

The further you progress through your degree, the more complex things can get. The reading list gets longer, the modules get tougher, and your degree can begin to feel impossible. You can sit through an entire lecture or seminar feeling like you're watching a movie in a foreign language without the subtitles on. On the outside, you're nodding and pretending that you understand it all. However, on the inside, you're wondering whether it is socially acceptable to curl up in a ball and cry. You keep re-reading your notes in your revision sessions about these complex concepts, but you still don't understand them. No matter how many times you read the words, they just won't go in. The disastrous result is you sitting in an exam hall looking at the questions in front of you, and your mind going completely blank. You don't understand a thing.

It doesn't have to be that way. Whenever you are studying something complex, stop and always remember to KISS… **Keep. It. Simple. Stupid.**

If you're trying to understand a complex concept, try and break it down into its most simple form. This technique is named after the physicist Richard Feynman, who received a Nobel Prize for his contributions to quantum electrodynamics (so he knew a thing or two about understanding complex ideas). Feynman was well known amongst his peers as the 'Great Explainer' for his ability to break down the seemingly complex into easily understandable ideas. The 'Feynman Technique' involves six simple steps that will make understanding those complex concepts a breeze.

How To Apply This At University – The Feynman Technique

1. **Write down the NAME of the concept** – Whatever topic you are learning about for your degree; write it down as the heading of the page.

2. **Write a SIMPLE one to two-page summary** – Break down the concept into its most simple form and avoid using any complicated language. Try and imagine that you are teaching it to another university student who studies an entirely different subject to you. Assume that they have no prior understanding of the subject. Try and use analogies, acronyms (i.e. KISS) and drawings. (Do not use any learning materials while doing this – it has to be done based purely on your own understanding!)

3. **Identify WEAK areas** – Read over your summary upon finishing it. Point out which areas you are the weakest on; these will be the areas that you struggled to explain or used complex language to do so.

4. **Go back to the LEARNING MATERIALS** – Fully digest the areas that you were weakest on.

5. **REPEAT the technique** – Once you have spent enough time visiting the learning materials so that you now understand the previously problematic areas, close the materials and repeat the technique, starting at the concept stage. Keep repeating until you can explain the whole concept in very clear and simple language. (To make the process easier, try and take on the mind of a five-year-old. Five-year-olds are fascinated by the world around them, they see everything as a question. The classic example is them pestering their parent with "Why? Why? Why? Why?" to every explanation they are given. Take on this five-year-old mindset with any assumptions you may have. Whenever you use complex language or make an assumption, keep asking yourself "why?" until you can explain it in its most simple form.)

6. **Get a STUDY-BUDDY** – The clichéd advice is true, the best way to learn is by teaching it to someone else. Break the concept down to a friend studying the same subject, or even better, someone who isn't, until they understand it. Get them to point out any parts that they don't understand as this will highlight the areas that you are weakest.

Uni Lifehacks: From 'Cutting Your Reading Time In Half', To 'How To Wake Up For 9 AM Lectures'

Cutting Your Reading Time In Half – Get more time in your day by using 'dead time' (like doing the washing up or walking to uni) to do your reading. Put your headphones in and have Siri or Google Translate read your readings for you. Just highlight all the text and press the 'read' button.

Seek Out Final Years – If you are a first or second year, before choosing your modules for the next year, befriend people in their final year who are studying the same degree. Get as much information you can about what are the easiest, hardest and most enjoyable module choices.

The Most Effective Flashcard System – Spaced repetition is one of the most useful tools to help remember something on your course. It works by repeating concepts on a staggered timeline until you are familiar with them. Follow this process:

A. Create flashcard headings with:
    - 'Check Everyday',
    - 'Check Every Other Day',
    - 'Check Every 7 Days'
    - 'Check Every 14 Days'
    - 'Check Every 28 Days'.

B. Every time you remember a flashcard from one of the headings, it gets bumped up to the next heading.

C. If you forget one of the flashcards from any of the headings, it gets moved all the way back down to 'Check Everyday'.

Freehand > Typing – When you write notes freehand, your brain has to process them before you put pen to paper. Most people can type far faster than they write, and it becomes an automatic process to just type what you hear, whether you understand it or not. Take the little bit of extra time to write it by hand and although you may have to fill in gaps where the lecturer went too fast, your understanding of the topic will be far better.

How To Write A First-Class Essay (Tips From First Class Graduates) – For this Lifehack, we decided to interview first class graduates who studied various degrees from English, Anthropology and Law, to Business and Psychology. Here's what they had to say:

A. *Use extra contact hours to get feedback* – Make sure you take advantage of your lecturer or tutor's office hours. They will often recommend sources for you to look at, and may even proofread your work if you ask nicely. Tip – record these contact hours on your phone's audio recorder so you can go over them later on and make a note of the main points they mentioned.

B. *Do the reading around the topic of your essay* – Anything that you don't understand, take note of it and bring it up in the office hour when you visit.

C. *Get feedback and correct your mistakes* – Insanity is said to be defined as *"doing the same thing over and over again and expecting a different result"*. No matter how hard you try, if you keep making the same mistakes, you'll never be able to improve. Always get as much feedback as you possibly can and try to correct your mistakes in the next essay. Have a list of points to improve on from the previous essay when you are writing your next one. Review thoroughly and create a checklist after finishing the first draft. Have you fixed those recurring errors? Check your grammar, your sources and your structure.

D. *Improve your written style* – Make use of any help you can get with your writing such as the Royal Literary Fund, which places writers in universities across the UK to help students develop their writing. Also, download a software like 'Grammarly', to get the edge on your writing and spot those innocent mistakes.

E. *Keep a copy of the marking criteria in front of you* – When you are planning, rewriting and redrafting your essay, keep checking the marking criteria! Check that you are meeting all the requirements they have set. The marker will have this in front of them when they are marking your essay, so you should have it in front of you when you're writing it.

F. *Ask a friend who gets good grades to give you feedback* – Look at how they prepare and write their essays. Ask for feedback on what you have written. Also, talk to people who are on the same course as you and discuss ideas or topics that relate to the module. It's good to have your arguments challenged, if you can show you have thought about strong counter-arguments to your position in your essay and have achieved a reasoned conclusion, you will be well rewarded.

How To Wake Up For 9 AM Lectures

A. *Place your phone across the room* – The hardest step in waking up early is getting out of bed. Having your phone blaring its alarm from across the room will definitely help with this! (Try putting the phone in a bowl or a glass to make the alarm louder.)

B. *Drink lots of water before bed* – This is an ancient technique that goes back way before alarm clocks. Your desire to hit the snooze button will be nothing in comparison to your need to go to the loo!

Housing & Housemates:
Heaven or Hell?

"Everybody wants to save the Earth;
nobody wants to help do the dishes."

–P.J. O'Rourke

"As you make your bed, so must you lie on it."

–Russian Proverb

How To Make The Perfect Housing Choice:
Picking The People And The Place

Followed by impending deadlines, horrific hangovers, and a negative bank balance, the recurring issue that students complain about the most is their housing. Whether it's mould in the house, 'that housemate' who keeps eating everyone's food or everybody avoiding their washing up, in one way or another, housing is always a point of contention for students. Therefore, before making any decision about where or whom to live with, give this section a read.

Choosing Your Housemates

Your housemates are going to be the people you spend the vast majority of your time with at university… Choose them wisely! It may seem odd to go into this much depth when thinking about who to live with; but making a mistake here could cost you dearly, so make sure you consider the following:

1. **Personality** – A lot of students decide to live with people because they lived with them in halls and now feel like they can't say no to them. Try and choose housemates who are similar to you and you get on well with. Try and avoid the people who are only your friends because you happen to have been placed near them in your first year or because they asked you first. It's better to have an awkward conversation and tell them you don't want to live with them now than spend the whole of next year living with the regret. Oh, and if they have any really annoying habits now, don't live with them! These habits will only get more annoying with time!

2. **Lifestyle** – Are your lifestyles similar or do they clash? One of the best parts of university is meeting a variety of people, but if your lifestyles clash it'll have an adverse impact on your life, meaning they aren't the ideal housemate for you. For example, if you are someone who likes to get up at 6 AM and start your day by hitting the gym, then you probably shouldn't live with someone who is 'on the sesh' every night and wakes you up at 4 AM when they get in.

3. **Cleanliness** – Even if you really like the person, but they never clean up and you're a clean freak, there will inevitably be some arguments when you live together. Similarly, if you're someone who is relaxed about cleanliness, you are going to struggle to live with someone who is a cleaning fanatic. The best way to

gauge someone's cleanliness is the classic 'bedroom test'. Look at their bedroom next time you are in there with them. If it looks like a bomb has just hit, they are probably not that fussed about cleanliness or being tidy. Similarly, if it is immaculate, they are probably very strict when it comes to keeping things spick and span.

4. **Romantic** – Everybody at university will eventually hear about a horror story involving couples who lived together. Of course, some couples manage to live together in complete harmony, but this is usually the exception rather than the rule. Don't try and play the odds. Instead just live apart. If you are living together and you suffer a break-up, it can turn quickly turn into an episode of *The Jeremy Kyle Show*. When you've just broken up with someone, you often want some time and space to yourself to move on. This will be difficult when you have to eat your cereal next to them each morning.

Choosing Your House

Once you have decided whom you are going to live with, you are going to want to start viewing houses or flats as soon as possible. The longer you leave it the less choice you will be left with, as all the good houses will be taken. Make sure you consider:

1. **Price** – Make a decision as a group, would you rather have the extra money or a better place to live? It will ultimately depend on you as individuals. Make sure you do your research properly and don't just assume that price is the only determining factor of value.

2. **Location** – Do you want it quiet? Do you want a garden? Would you rather live near the nightlife? Live nearer the university? Ask yourself these sorts of questions.

3. **Landlord** – If they don't get rid of the mould in your room or if they try to keep your deposit without a valid reason, no house, or landlord, is worth the hassle. But how do you know all this in advance? The best way is to ask the current tenants. This is probably the most important piece of practical advice about uni housing: before signing anything, go back to the house without the landlord there, speak to the current tenants and ask them about all the real pros and cons of the house and the landlord. These students have first-hand experience of what the property is really like, and aren't trying to sell you anything unlike the landlord or the estate agents are!

4. **Neighbours** – If you like to have house parties and play your music loud, you're not going to want to live in a non-student residential area. My house made this mistake and got two noise complaints in the first week of living there! Similarly, if you are an 'early to bed, early to rise' kind of person, you are probably not going to want to live in a student area that is known for its Project X-esque house parties. It's quite hard to motivate yourself to go for an early morning jog when the 'after-sesh' next door has just begun.

Uni Lifehacks: From 'Cleaning A Bathroom In Half The Time', To 'Ironing Without An Iron'

Cleaning A Bathroom In Half The Time:

A. *Cleaning a shower head* – Fill up a zip lock bag with vinegar and soak the showerhead overnight. Remove in the morning and scrub away the remaining dirt.

B. *Cleaning shower mould:*

1. Put undiluted vinegar and/or baking soda into a spray bottle and spray onto the mould. (Leave for 45 minutes)

2. Scrub hard with a brush and rinse the surface.

3. Re-spray with vinegar.

C. *Unblocking a toilet:*

1. Put some towels around the toilet and make sure it is not near overfilling (If so, scoop some water out.)

2. Apply two squirts of dishwashing liquid into the blocked bowl. Then pour some hot water into the bowl (Make sure it doesn't overflow!)

3. Wait for 25 minutes. Upon return, the water should have gone down considerably.

4. Pour a bucket of hot water into the bowl and wait two minutes, then flush the toilet.

Make Your House Smell Of Cinnamon – Hoover up three table-spoons of cinnamon before vacuuming the rest of the house to create a cinnamon smell wherever you go.

Getting Sick Out Of A Carpet:

1. Scoop up and bin as much as you can.

2. Soak remaining stain with lukewarm water.

3. Mix baking soda with water and spread the mix until it covers the sick. Leave for 10-15 minutes and hoover it up.

4. If there's any left, leave baking soda mix overnight and hoover it up the next day.

5. If caused by a friend, re-evaluate your friendship and consider blocking their number for the foreseeable future.

The Ultimate Laundry Cheat Sheet:

A. *Stop your dirty clothes from smelling* – Place a bar of scented soap in your laundry basket to keep your dirty clothes and room smelling fresh.

B. *Use a towel to speed up drying time* – Throw in a dry fluffy towel when you are drying clothes in a tumble dryer, and it will speed up drying time. (Take the towel out after ten to fifteen minutes for it to be effective. Otherwise, the towel will keep the moisture in.)

C. *Unshrinking clothing with conditioner* – Mix some lukewarm water with hair conditioner. Then put the shrunk clothing in the mixture and leave for fifteen minutes. This will help stretch out the fibres. Wrap the item in a towel and give it a squeeze. Place the item on a towel and gently stretch out the item to the desired length. Let the item dry, and it will soon be back to its original size.

D. *Never lose socks or underwear* – Socks and underwear often go missing in a uni student's wash, leaving you worse for wear at the end of term. Avoid this happening by keeping your socks and underwear separate in a laundry bag, and then throwing the bag in the wash so you never lose them.

E. *The lazy student's quick wash* – If you are in a rush and you haven't had time to properly wash the outfit you wore last night – try this: Throw your outfit in the dryer with 3-6 ice cubes. Roll up a ball of tinfoil and throw it in the dryer too. Turn the dryer on the highest setting for 10-15 minutes and your outfit will be much fresher and ready to go.

F. *Removing fabric balls* – Get rid of the annoying balls of fabric (pilling) on your clothes by gently scraping a disposable razor over the top.

Ironing Without An Iron

A. *The shower steam iron* – Hang your clothes on a hanger on the back of your bathroom door and shut it. Have a hot, ten-minute shower, and then gently stretch out all the wrinkles. (*This is best for larger items like shirts and trousers.*)

B. *The hair dryer iron* – Simply stretch the (slightly) damp and wrinkled item of clothing gently on a flat surface and move the hairdryer up and down in the direction you have stretched. The heat from the hairdryer will get rid of the biggest creases, leaving you with a relatively crease-free item in less than two minutes. (*This is best for smaller items like t-shirts.*)

3

The Student Chef's Cheat Sheet

"No one is born a great cook, one learns by doing."

–Julia Child

"My grandma can do better than that… And she's dead!"

–Gordon Ramsay

5 Mouth-Watering Student Recipes With Mob Kitchen

Eating well and maintaining a healthy lifestyle isn't a top priority for most students; despite concern and advice from parents, diet is an often neglected area. One of the main issues for students on a budget is that buying and cooking fresh food can be seen as an unnecessary evil – it is expensive, time-consuming and doesn't always produce the Michelin quality meal you were hoping for. Viral stars Mob Kitchen *(FB: @mobkitchen, IG: @mobkitchenuk, www.mobkitchen.co.uk)* have taken it upon themselves to show anyone how to make delicious, healthy, affordable food. To pass on some of their culinary wisdom, we collaborated with them for this part of the book. The recipes are all costed by the jar/tin/pack, and the only things they expect you to have at home are salt, pepper and olive oil. Their goal is to help you 'Feed 4 for £10'; so here's a selection of their best student recipes:

EGG MOBMUFFIN

INGREDIENTS

Red Chillies – £0.60
Bunch of Chives – £0.70
1 Lemon – £0.30
4 White English Muffins – £0.50
Smoked Streaky Bacon – £2.00
10 Eggs – £2.20
2 Large Avocados – £2.00

Total Cost – £8.30

METHOD

1. Preheat the oven to 180°C/356°F.
2. Put bacon on a rack and whack it in the oven until crispy (or however you like it)
3. Guac time – Put two avocados, a chopped chilli, a handful of chopped chives and the juice of a lemon into a bowl. Add salt, pepper and olive oil, and mash.
4. Fry your eggs.
5. Toast your buns.
6. Build – Bun, guac, egg, bacon, bun, guac, bacon, bun. Tuck in and enjoy.

GODFATHER MEATBALLS

INGREDIENTS

Casarecce Pasta *(Should be able to find in all large supermarkets. If not, penne or a shell paste will work fine.)* – £0.59

Balsamic Vinegar – £1.00

Chilli Flakes – £0.85

Tinned Tomatoes *(You want to use the good ones in this recipe)* – £1.90

Parmesan – £2.00

Garlic – £0.30

Basil – £0.70

Sausages – £2.50

Total Cost – £9.84

METHOD

1. Take your sausages. Cut a little slit in the skin, and then squeeze out the meat. Make that meat into little balls. Roughly three balls per sausage.

2. Fry your balls until they have browned on all sides (roughly 2 minutes on each side on a medium heat). Don't jiggle them about too much or else they will break up.

3. Once browned, add 3 cloves of sliced garlic and a healthy splash of balsamic vinegar.

4. Once the garlic has softened, but not browned, add half your basil leaves and another splash of vinegar.

5. When they have wilted, add two tins of tomatoes. Half fill the tins with water and pour into the sauce.

6. Bring to the boil, and then simmer until the sauce has thickened, reducing roughly by half. This should take around 15 minutes.

7. Cook your pasta in salted water. Once cooked, add it to the sauce. Mix it all together, and serve with remaining basil, grated parmesan and more chilli flakes (if you like it spicy!)

VEGETABLE CURRY

INGREDIENTS

2 Aubergines – £1.30

Ginger – £0.27

Garlic – £0.30

Coriander – £0.70

Cumin – £0.85

Cayenne Pepper – £0.85

Chopped Tomatoes – £0.70

2 Brown Onions – £0.32

2 Sweet Potatoes – £0.66

Spinach – £1.00

Yeo Valley Yoghurt – £1.50

Turmeric – £0.85

Chickpeas – £0.50

Total Cost: £9.80

METHOD

1. Finely chop knob of ginger, three cloves of garlic and your onions. Fry off the ginger and the garlic, adding 3 teaspoons of turmeric, 3 teaspoons of cumin and 1 teaspoon of cayenne pepper.

2. Add chopped onions. Allow them to soften.

3. Cube your sweet potatoes and aubergines. Add them to the pan. Coat them in the spices and oil.

4. Add tins of chopped tomatoes. Then, fill both tins with water and add the water. Bring to the boil, then stir and cover with a lid. Leave at a gentle simmer for 45 minutes.

5. After 45 minutes add chickpeas. Put the lid back on. Leave for 15 more minutes.

6. Then, add spinach and coriander stalks. Put the lid back on for 3 more minutes.

7. Remove curry from the heat.

8. Allow to cool slightly, and then add your yoghurt. This will prevent curdling. Marble the yoghurt through the curry, and then scatter remaining coriander leaves on top.

CHORIZO AND GNOCCHI BAKE

INGREDIENTS

Crushed Chillies – £0.85

Parmesan – £2.00

Mozzarella – £1.50

Chopped Tomatoes – £0.31

Spinach – £1.00

Basil – £1.00

Garlic – £0.30

Chorizo – £2.50

500g Gnocchi – £0.75

Total Cost – £9.91

METHOD

1. Finely chop 2 cloves of garlic and chop chorizo into nuggets.

2. Place chorizo in frying pan and cook until crispy. Then add garlic, a teaspoon of chilli flakes and a handful of basil leaves. Cook for 30 seconds, and then add 200g of spinach. Wilt the spinach down, and then pour in a tin of chopped tomatoes. Fill the tin halfway with water, and pour that in. Turn sauce onto a medium heat and allow to reduce and thicken.

3. While the sauce is thickening, put your gnocchi into a bowl and cover with boiling water.

4. Once the sauce has thickened remove from the heat.

5. Drain the gnocchi and pour it into a baking dish. Cover the gnocchi with your chorizo sauce. Flatten it out, and then tear two balls of mozzarella over the top. Cover the whole dish with grated Parmesan, and then place under the grill for 15 minutes or until the cheese is golden and bubbling. Serve and enjoy!

SPICED VEGGIE GYROS

INGREDIENTS

1 Cucumber – £0.50

Bunch of Mint – £0.70

Pot of Yoghurt – £0.90

4 Pittas – £0.50

Cayenne Pepper – £0.85

1 Red Onion – £0.17

2 Peppers (Not Green) – £1.00

Garlic – £0.30

1 Lemon – £0.30

Pomegranate Seeds – £1.00

Garam Masala – £0.85

400g Chickpeas – £0.50

3 Courgettes – £1.13

1 Cauliflower – £1.00

Total Cost – £9.70

METHOD

1. Preheat oven to 180°C/356°F.

2. Finely chop courgettes, red onion and pepper into bite-size pieces. Break cauliflower up into little florets. Place into a baking tray. Pour in a tin of chickpeas, with some of the starchy water. Pour over a good splash of olive oil, add two heaped teaspoons of cayenne pepper, two heaped teaspoons of garam masala, a sprinkle of salt and pepper, and mix everything together. Place in oven for 30 minutes.

3. Tzatziki time. Pour the pot of yoghurt into a bowl. Add a small bunch of finely chopped mint, the juice of one lemon, and one grated cucumber. Grate in a clove of garlic, season well and mix it all together.

4. After 30 minutes, remove vegetables from oven, mix them about, and then place back in the oven for 15 more minutes.

5. Assembly time. Take a warm pitta. Load it with your spiced vegetables, then tzatziki, then some pomegranate seeds, then some more vegetables, more tzatziki, more pomegranate seeds, and TUCK IN!

Uni Lifehacks: From '7 Game Changing Items Most Students Don't Have In Their Kitchen', To 'How To Never Have An Argument With Your Flatmates About Washing Up'

7 Game Changing Items Most Students Don't Have In Their Kitchen – Here are some little gems that the average student doesn't have, or only finds out about late into their university career:

A. *Blender* – It takes absolutely no cooking skills to make a smoothie. It's a super easy way to get your protein, fruit and vegetable requirements on days that they are lacking. The clean up afterwards is super quick too.

B. *George Foreman Grill* – This grill has reportedly sold over 100,000,000 units since its invention in 1994! It isn't a surprise; the grill makes cooking so easy that any hungry person could make a meal on it, even the most amateur student chef. With this you can cook anything from a full English to toasties, to burgers and steaks – all you have to do is chuck it on the grill.

C. *Non-stick Wok* – This is the godfather of pans. It is by far the most versatile pan out there, and you can cook up a tonne of dishes with this piece of kit The non-stick factor means it is really easy to clean too.

D. *Crock-Pot* – Also known as a 'Slow Cooker' because it takes six to eight hours to cook your meals in. Simply chuck your ingredients in before you go the library or before you go to bed at night. Upon your return, you will be met with an amazing smell and food that is worthy of a Michelin star by student standards. And, in one large pot, you can make enough meals to last you a week.

E. *Tupperware* – If you are regularly eating out or buying food, you will be in 'the red' way before the end of term. Getting into the habit of making packed lunches the night before will save you a fortune at university.

F. *Mini Fridge* – Shared fridges can be a nightmare. Keep your precious items to yourself in a nice clean fridge, ideally close enough to reach without leaving your bed.[4]

G. *Dishmatic* – What is it? It's a sponge on a stick that you put washing up liquid and water into. Google it – it will change your washing up experience. [5]

Become Twice As Good In The Kitchen By Downloading This App
– Lots of students end up repeating the same meals because they can't be bothered with the effort it takes to learn how to cook something new. Download SideChef, which provides you with step-by-step photos, instructions and voice commands for over 2,500 recipes. The app also has an integrated timer and specific instruction videos.

How To Never Have A Washing Up Argument With Your Flatmates:

*"If you never had an argument about washing up in a
student house – did you really ever live in a student house?"*

– PLATO[6]

Everyone does their own washing up when they start living together. Nobody intentionally goes out of their way to stop this pattern (you'd like to think!) However, as people start getting more and

---

[4] Be careful, some landlords and student accommodations won't allow you to have a fridge in your room, so check first.

[5] Check out Mob Kitchen's insight for more suggestions.

[6] This is not an actual Plato quote.

more hungover or find themselves in a rush to get to lectures, the kitchen gradually gets messier and people 'forget' which items are theirs. Resulting in a massive pile of washing up next to the sink, and nobody wanting to deal with it. My flat had countless arguments about washing up, so we built a system that ensured we never had any arguments about the washing up ever again.

Adios Mess, Hello Cleanliness

1. *Tape off areas* – Create separate areas on counters by the sink, designating each taped off area to a different housemate (the area will need to be wide enough to fit large pans.)

2. *Safe zones* – If the person doesn't have time to do their washing up, they can leave it in their area until they do have time. This area becomes their safe zone for a set time period, and nobody can criticise them for leaving anything in their zone for the agreed time period.

3. *48 hour rule* – It is an 'unwritten rule' that the person has to do the washing up in their area within the next 48 hours or has to deal with a 'punishment' from the rest of the house. (First round at the pub on your next outing?)

After implementing this system, the people in our flat had accountability for their washing up. Nobody ever had to wash up an item that wasn't theirs again. If somebody started to let their washing up slip, everyone could see that they weren't washing as it was all in their individual labelled area. Whenever they walked past their filthy area, they would be reminded that it was *theirs* and needing doing. It also gives everyone a bit of freedom to leave their washing up for a short period of time if they can't wash it up straight away.

How To Cut Your Washing Up In Half – When you are feeling lazy, put cling film over your plates before you put food on them. When you are finished, put the cling film in the bin, and your plate won't need to be washed up. Or alternatively, just use paper plates. You can get a pack of 100 for £4.50 online.

All Natural Microwave Cleaner That Leaves It Smelling Fresh:

1. Cut a lemon in half and squeeze the juice out into a bowl.

2. Take the halves of lemon and put them face down into the bowl.

3. Put the bowl in the microwave and set for four minutes.

4. After the four minutes is up, leave the microwave door shut for a further four minutes to keep the lemony steam inside.

5. Open the microwave door, remove the bowl and wipe down the inside of the microwave.

6. Enjoy your citrus-fresh microwave!

Ridding Fridges Of Nasty Smells – If your fridge constantly smells, remove the offending item and wipe down any liquid remnants of it. Then slice up some citrus fruits and leave them in the refrigerator for 2-3 days.

Step Up Your Ice Cube Game – Do you want a chilled glass of wine but don't want to water it down with ice cubes? Put some grapes in your ice tray, use those instead and hey presto, chilled wine with no added water. Alternatively, if you are you are looking to drink your body weight in water to repent for last night's sins, chuck some blueberries and strawberries in the ice cube tray. Ice-berries plus bottle of water equals delicious, ice-cold, flavoured water.

PART TWO

MONEY

Hip Hop legend, *Notorious B.I.G.* once famously said "Mo Money, Mo Problems." It's safe to say many students do not echo this sentiment. Money, or rather lack of it, is a prevalent issue for students across the U.K. The money issue manifests itself in different ways, but a familiar story plays out a bit like this:

1. Student gets their student loan.

2. Student lives like a king or queen for a couple of weeks.

3. Student realises their money's completely gone, or has been poorly budgeted, or wasn't enough in the first place.

4. Student struggles to make ends meet for the rest of the term.

Although students are notorious for being penniless (of course everybody's financial situation is different), it *is* possible to survive and live above the breadline, as this part of the book will demonstrate.

Chapter Four focuses on how you can save not just mere pennies, but potentially thousands of pounds at university, outlining a bunch of ways you can save money, including the best money-related apps and plugins for students (don't worry they are all free, or else this would be slightly counterintuitive.)

After learning how to minimise your student expenditure in the fourth chapter, the fifth chapter builds on this by showing you how to maximise your student income. It gives a breakdown of six unconventional ways of making money which most students aren't aware of. Finally, in Chapter Six, we cover the six key steps you can take to help ensure you get your dream graduate job by detailing a guide to help make your CV stand out, and shine in an interview. As well as a Lifehack for you to get the CEO's e-mail address and some of the best LinkedIn tips and tricks around.

4

Staying Out Of Your Overdraft

"We didn't actually overspend our budget. The allocation simply fell short of our expenditure."

–Keith Davis

"I have enough money to last me the rest of my life, unless I buy something."

–Jackie Mason

5 Free Apps And Browser Plugins That Will Revolutionise Your Uni Finances

Keeping on top of your finances at university is something you know you should do, but there are often so many other more exciting things on your to-do list that you never get around to doing it. Then, fast forward to a point in the future when you inevitably go to pay via card in a public place, only to find out your card has been rejected! You then frantically check your bank balance and you are flabbergasted as to where all your money has gone. Here are some apps and plugins, which are going to help stop that nightmare from happening:

1. **Splitwise** – One of the most common causes of arguments between friends and housemates at university is money, in particular, who owes what to whom. Splitwise lets you add all of your housemates or friends to a group on the app, and then subsequently split your bills and track who owes what. You can also input the dates when bills are due so that one friend who conveniently 'forgets' to pay will receive reminders and won't have any excuse to not pay. (Alternative apps include Circle, Level and Splittable.)

   Available on: App Store and Google Play

2. **Honey** – Student life, given the amount of free time you have, often involves a lot of online shopping. Whenever you are at checkout, Honey will search the internet for discount codes and will automatically apply them.

   Available on: Chrome, FireFox, Safari

3. **Price Blink** – There is no point spending £150 on those flights to Budapest when they were available for £75 elsewhere. However, searching for the best possible deal can be boring and take hours. You will also always wonder whether there is a better deal out there than the one you have found. Price Blink is a free plugin that will notify you to lower prices on whatever you are looking at and will provide a direct link to the cheapest option available online.

   Available on: Chrome, Firefox, Safari

4. **Monzo** – A study found that physically handling cash when you pay for something actually triggers emotional pain, whereas paying with a card does not! (3) Avoid the disconnect between

your imagined bank balance and your actual bank balance, by being aware and reminded of how much you are spending. Once a fortnight spend five minutes looking at your outgoings from the last two weeks. Prepaid debit cards like Monzo make you "top up" your debit card with money from another account, which will force you to budget effectively. It also breaks down your spending habits, so be warned, you might find out that you spend more on that end of the night takeaway than you previously thought! (Alternative apps include Spending Tracker and Fudget.)

5. **ATM Hunter** – This uses geolocation to look for the nearest ATMs and gives you directions to them.

    Available on: App Store and Google Play

Uni Lifehacks: From 'Get All The Best Student Discounts', To 'Saving Thousands Of Pounds By Leaving One Item At Home On A Night Out'

Get All The Best Student Discounts:

- Apple – 10% off
- ASOS – 10% off
- Boots – £5 eye test and 10% off glasses over £100
- Boohoo – 10% off
- Co-Operative – 10% off
- McDonald's – Free Medium Fries with a Big Mac or Chicken sandwich OR show your student card when you buy a meal and they will give you a free hamburger, cheeseburger or McFlurry
- Megabus – 10% off
- National Express – 25% off coach travel with NUS extra on some journeys
- Odeon – Student Prices are 25% off with NUS extra Monday – Thursday
- Pizza Hut – 20% Off
- Spotify – 50% off premium with NUS Extra
- Urban Outfitters – 10% off
- Topshop – 10% off
- *Download Student Beans and Unidays for additional discounts

Get ⅓ Of All Your Train Journeys – The 16-25 Railcard is available to anyone who is aged between 16-25 who is in full-time education. It's £30 per year, and you get 1/3 discount on all fares. (You can also get 12% off your Railcard if you show your student card.)

Switch Banks At The Start Of Each Academic Year – See Owen Burek's insight from Save The Student! on page 268.

Saving Thousands Of Pounds By Leaving One Item At Home On A Night Out – A friend of mine went on a night out with the intention of spending £20; only to wake up the next morning to find a debit card receipt that showed that he had bought a round for everyone at the bar (including a £160 bottle of Moët!)

Avoid overspending on a night out by not giving your inebriated self the ability to do it in the first place. Leave your card at home and just take out £20 instead[7]. (Taxi is £2.50 each way and entry is up to £5. You then have around £10 for drinks.)

The Maths Of Leaving Your Debit Card At Home

For example, if you end up spending an average of **£10 more than you planned every time you go out** with your debit card; (from our experience, you will likely spend more than £10, but let's be conservative) and you go out 1-3 times a week over a 12-week term, this equates to:

£120-£360 a term

£360-£1,080 a year

£1,080-£3,240 over three years at university!

Don't Bin It, Freeze It – The average UK household bin contains around £450 worth of uneaten food each year (2). It's probably even more for students as items can often get lost in a shared fridge.

---

[7] The numbers may be different for students living in London. Also, if you don't take your card out, make sure you take precautions and stay with your friends.

Extend the shelf life by freezing it. (Obviously, not all food can be frozen, but meat, bread, and prepared meals are easy to freeze and save space and waste.)

Try And Get Books For Free Instead Of Buying Them – Check out Google Scholar and the library before buying a book. See if it is available for free, or if you can, request a section to read before you splurge on buying the whole book. Some academic books and textbooks are costly, and looking at Google Scholar or in the library before buying it could save you buying five or six each year. Over the course of your degree, this could easily add up to a saving of a couple of hundred pounds.

Hunt Out Hidden Bargains – Check out swap shops, second-hand buy/sell markets and local hidden bargain stores. Students who no longer need items or don't want to take things with them when they move away will be looking to sell all kinds of items, from event tickets to laptops. Also, check out second-hand sales websites like Gumtree and eBay. To maximise your bargain hunting, check out tools such as 'local eBay deals mapper' which is software that scouts out the best eBay deals nearby.

Do Not Get A TV licence – Let's be clear, this is not for one moment suggesting that you should forgo paying for a TV licence and watch it anyway. That is illegal, and it would land us in lots of trouble. Instead, it is saying that you don't need to watch live TV in the first place. Just watch anything you want (so long as it isn't on the BBC) on catch up and On Demand services, rather than forking out your share of the £145.50 a year cost of a TV licence.

A Piece Of Plastic Which Could Save You Up To £1,800 Across Your Time At Uni – If you eat lunch out three times a week and spend £5 each time, you will spend an extra £15 every week. Although this may not seem like much at the time, it equates to around £600 a year and £1,800 across three years (depending on how long your terms are). Invest in some Tupperware, do some weekly meal preparation or use leftovers, and if you want hot food, buy a flask!

Get Amazon Prime Free For Six Months – Use Amazon Prime's six-month free student trial. This gives you unlimited one-day delivery on millions of items, unlimited streaming of thousands of TV shows and much more. Be aware though, it doesn't cancel automatically and will rollover if you forget. If you continue after six months, you get a 50% discount too (it should be £79 per year; it's £39 per year for students.) It enables you to have multiple bank cards on one account so you could save money by splitting one account with your flatmates.

Shop Quicker And Avoid Queues – If you don't have anything in your diary during these times, do your shopping on weekday mornings and Friday evenings. These are the days that people have much better things to be doing than shopping, so the shops will be the quietest.

Own Brands > Name Brands – Own brands cost less and are often made in the same factories as branded products. A recent study by Harvard Business Review showed that on average consumers rated them as tasting better than the name brands! (4)

Plan Your Meals And Work Backwards – Instead of going to the shop wondering what to buy, plan your meals for the week and have a list of things that you need to buy. This will reduce your spending considerably as you won't be tempted to impulse buy.

Visit Costco At The Start Of Term – If your parents have a membership, or you know anyone with one, it's worthwhile just before the start of every term to stock up on all your essential items. Particularly the following: toilet roll, kitchen roll, washing up liquid and soap. You'll be able to get it at a bulk discount, which will save you money, and it will also come in very handy… Finding out you have run out of toilet roll is never a fun experience.

Never Food Shop On An Empty Stomach – A research study found that participants who were hungry spent 64% more money on shopping than those who weren't (5). (The study measured appliance shopping and not food shopping; just imagine what the results would be like at a supermarket!) The reason why you are more likely to spend money when hungry is that the stomach releases a hormone called ghrelin which affects the clarity of decision-making and level of impulsiveness. By shopping when you're not hungry, you will save an impressive amount of money. Plus, your shopping basket is likely to be a lot healthier too.

More Money, Less Problems

"My problem lies in reconciling my
gross habits with my net income."

–Errol Flynn

"Money frees you from doing things you dislike. Since I
dislike doing nearly everything, money is handy."

–Groucho Marx

The Student Hustler's Guide: 6 Ways Of Making Money Which Most Students Don't Know About

We're not going to insult your intelligence. You don't gain anything from being told to go and work behind a bar, drive for Deliveroo or wait tables. These jobs are the norm for uni students; we didn't want to talk about the traditional ways students make money, most of which you were already aware of. Instead, below are a list of jobs and mini-businesses which are little known amongst the student community. Not only are they different, but they'll also often come with much better pay, more flexible hours, they'll look amazing on your CV, and you'll learn valuable skills as a result.

1. **Ambassador** – Major brands from Spotify to Red Bull to Bacardi are looking for brand ambassadors in student cities to promote their products. They'll most likely ask you to do promotional activities every week, whether it's sponsoring a house party or running a pop-up stall at the student union.

    You could also end up running events, coordinating groups of different people and developing your time management skills – all of which are valuable to future employers! Do your research on what companies have brand ambassadors in your city and which the best ones are.

    There's also the potential of becoming an ambassador for your university too. Tasks will vary from calling up members of the alumni to touring A-level students and their parents around campus. Not only are the hours super flexible, but you are already at uni most days, so the travel is minimal.

2. **Tutoring** – The fact that you are at university shows you have the necessary qualifications to start this little venture. There are lots of anxious parents and teenagers out there who are looking for help in achieving the same feats that you have. You have a valuable skill in this situation. You have recently completed the very same A-Levels, meaning you know them well; you are young so you can relate to the student; you have proven that you can pass them – there are plenty of unique selling points here! (David used to tutor GCSE students and charged over £15 per hour; he had to turn away business because he was so busy!) The real benefit here is that because you are a uni student, you can undercut the teachers and lecturers that are already tutoring in your area, meaning more business for you, and a steady stream of students. Parents talk; if you can get their

kid the results they need, your name will spread like wildfire. Free marketing!

Here are some websites to start with: *www.tutorhunt.co.uk*, *www.tutora.co.uk* and *www.mytutor.co.uk*.

3. **Freelancing** – Whatever valuable skill you have; charge for it. Love to DJ and know there are lots of house parties nearby? Get paid to perform. Know a foreign language? Become a language teacher. Play a musical instrument? Teach music. Handy with a camera? Become a photographer for nightclubs or weddings. Clean freak? Set up a cleaning business for student houses – now there's a profitable business idea! There are loads of other niche skills that you can sell. For example, I knew a guy at university who was a talented artist and loved drawing. He sold his portraits and sketches to other students, he offered drawings unique to the buyer, which gave him a unique selling point and provided value to his customers. Think of some skills you have, or you could easily develop, and how you can turn them into a service or product that you can offer to people in exchange for money.

4. **Social Media Consulting** – There are so many businesses that are run by members of older generations who haven't a clue how to use social media effectively. The first step: educate yourself in Facebook and Instagram marketing, and SEO (Search Engine Optimisation – making websites appear higher up the rankings in a Google search). It's easy to learn, with thousands of free educational videos on YouTube as well as many other online resources. When you acquire enough knowledge you can offer your services to businesses; you will be surprised to learn how many businesses are not taking advantage of social media. Make sure you prepare your pitch by researching their company and show them the value you can offer them. Interview their target market demographic and find out what the business could be

doing better. Show the business the value you can add. To try and entice the first few clients, offer to do it for free initially, you will build up experience and positive referrals that will then help attract paying customers.

5. **Matched Betting**[8] – Matched betting removes the risk from betting. In its simplest terms, you play bookies (like Ladbrokes) and a betting exchange (like Betfair) against each other. Using the 'free bet' offers that betting exchanges give out to new customers, you can negate the risk of losing money by backing the opposite of the bet you placed with the bookies. It seems complex, but here's an example. If you put a bet on with Ladbrokes on Liverpool to win at 2/1, using the free bet you would put money on Liverpool drawing or losing. That way, regardless of whether you win or lose your original bet, your other one will come through.[9]

6. **Nude Art Model** – Okay, this one definitely isn't for everyone but hear us out. Pay is roughly £10 an hour, it's a funny anecdote, and you literally have to do nothing. Your entire job is sitting or standing still. Not only that, if you have narcissistic tendencies, you've got a self-portrait to hang on the wall!

---

[8] Please gamble responsibly and don't blow your whole student loan – *www.begambleaware.co.uk*

[9] For more detail, check out *www.savethestudent.org/make-money/what-is-matched-betting* and *www.savethestudent.org/make-money* for more money making tips.

Uni Lifehacks: From 'Making Cash By Selling Your Old Stuff Online', To 'How To Come Up With An Idea For Your First Business'

Making Money By Selling Your Old Stuff Online – Look at the items that you've not used in the last month – ask yourself "*Do I really need this?*" If the answer isn't yes, sell it. Try eBay, Gumtree, Depop or Facebook Buy/Sell groups.

Scratch Your Flatmates' Backs – Offer to do your flatmates' chores for cash. (e.g. wash their dishes, take out the bins, do their shopping, cook their meals, proofread their essays or clean their rooms.)

Buy Tickets ASAP – How can buying something help you make money? Well, if you decide to go to the event, ticket prices get more and more expensive nearer to the date, meaning the later you leave it, the more you pay. If you decide not to go to the event, you can sell the ticket on or before the night for at least the original buying price and usually for much more. I know a guy who made cash every other night by buying tickets for him and a few friends for each event, and if his friends backed out of the night, he would sell the tickets and make a tidy profit.

Get Paid To Answer Questions – Fill out online surveys. The following companies will pay you or give you free vouchers or products to fill out their surveys. Try Swagbucks, Crowdology and Toluna.

Become A Human Guinea Pig – There will be research happening on campus by science departments who will often pay for participants. Sign up. (Be careful though, two students at Northumbria University signed up for a study on caffeine, and it nearly killed them because the test was conducted so monumentally wrongly. They were supposed to have 300mg of caffeine and ended up with

30g – equivalent to 100 cups of coffee, and double the dosage that usually kills people!)

Get Paid To Hang Out With Dogs – Miss your dog at home and short of change? Kill two birds with stone and offer to dog walk. Look for Facebook groups and dog walking apps.

A Collection Of The Best Job Websites:

A. Freelance/Part time – *www.studentjob.co.uk, www.studentgems.co.uk, www.indeed.co.uk*

B. Promotional work – *www.stuckforstaff.com*

C. Retail – *www.inretail.co.uk*

D. On-campus work – Check your university's website

E. Events – *www.eventstaffing.co.uk*

How To Come Up With An Idea For Your First Business At Uni:

A. *Look at your everyday problems* – The best business ideas are the ones that solve real world problems, and the worst business ideas are the ones that don't. Every time you have a problem, be mindful of it, write it down and try to think of a solution. If you are having that problem, it is likely that many other people are having the same problem too, meaning that they will pay for a solution if you find a cost-effective one.

B. *Listen to people's complaints* – Another way of identifying problems to solve is by listening to people's everyday complaints and writing them down.

C. *Write down 10 ideas every day* – Don't wait for your lightbulb moment to happen; instead, go out and make it happen. The 'idea muscle' is like any other muscle and needs regular practice to grow and become stronger.

The Maths Of The '10 Ideas A Day' Practice

If you come up with 10 ideas every day, it equates to **3650 ideas a year.**

Even if 99% of them are absolute garbage, that still leaves 1%, which is **36.5 good ideas. That's 35.5 ideas more than you need!** (6)

The Best Places To Get Funding For Your Business Idea:

A. *Contact your careers department* – They may be hosting funding competitions or have connections in the Alumni related to your particular market.

B. *NACUE* – Offers a £10,000 equity free cash prize every year to student businesses.

C. *Prince's Trust* – Offers financial help and business support to entrepreneurs aged 18-30

D. *Shell LiveWIRE* – Offers free business support and funding as well as being 'one of the UK's biggest online communities for young entrepreneurs.'

Become The 1% Of The Graduate Job Market

"It is said that the present is pregnant with the future."

–Voltaire

"One of the most common mistakes for an entry-level job interview is to take the position: 'What is this job going to do for me?' You should be saying 'Here's what I can do and here's what I want to do to help you."

–Norah O'Donnell

Getting Your Dream Graduate Job: Making Your CV Stand Out And Impressing In The Interview

Nearly 40% of graduates are looking for a job six months after graduation, and 25% are still unemployed after a year (7). To ensure you're not part of these statistics, you're going to want to stand out from all the other graduates you're competing against when it comes to your CV and job interview. The steps laid out below are what the majority of people you will be competing with don't do, and as a result, following them will give you a competitive advantage when it comes to finding a job after university.

Making Your CV Stand Out

1. **Talk To People Who Have Experience Within The Company** – Before you even start writing your CV, find out more about the job you are applying for from the people who have first-hand experience in the industry or company that you are looking to work in after university. You are going to want to get as much information about the hiring process that exists in this industry or company and what to do to help make your CV stand out. There are two ways of getting hold of this information:

   A. *Online* – For many large companies, there is information online about their recruitment process and what qualities they are looking for in an employee. A great starter resource to find out more information is *www.glassdoor.co.uk* – 'Glassdoor holds a growing database of millions of company reviews, CEO approval ratings, salary reports, interview reviews and questions, benefits reviews, office photos and more.'

   B. *Former or current employees* – Find someone who previously or currently works for the company (or within the industry) you are looking to apply for and message them politely asking to buy them a coffee so you can learn from them about the company. A good way to find these people is through your university alumni network or searching the company on LinkedIn. Once you meet them in person, try to ask them specific questions about the CV and interview process. Try and get as much direct and practical advice as you can. Also, this exercise can be a great networking tool as they may be able to put in a good word for you or introduce you to one of their contacts.

2. **Don't List Facts; Show Value** – Think long and hard about the type of employee that the company wants to hire. Reverse engineer it and create that narrative about yourself in your CV. Ramit Sethi, a bestselling author and employability expert, states that after twenty seconds of reading your CV, you should have already conveyed to the potential employer that you are the type of employee they are seeking. Don't just list facts about yourself; instead turn these facts into valuable skills in the eyes of the employer.

Showing Value In Your CV

Consider the two CV examples of **Person A** (who states facts) and **Person B** (who frames these facts as valuable skills in the eye of the employer):

Person A – University of Loughborough, 2015-2018, BSc, Business & Psychology, 2:1

Person B – University of Loughborough, 2015-2018, BSc, Business & Psychology. Coursework included social media marketing, consumer psychology, data analysis, entrepreneurship and persuasion.'

Person A's CV doesn't stand out from the crowd. They have merely stated the fact that they have a degree. Person B's CV, however, does. They have not just stated that they have a degree; they've also referenced the skill sets and knowledge they gained from their degree, all of which would provide value to the company. (8)

3.   **Keep It Short and Sweet** – A CV is not the time for waffle; you are going to want to communicate all the key information and cut the fat. The vast majority of graduate CV's take up two to three pages. Try and aim to get your CV on one page. It should be able to be read within one to two minutes. This will force you to focus on communicating the essential information to the reader. The person reading is no doubt busy, and usually has a pile of CV's to read through, and so they are likely to skim read your CV. Keep it short and sweet and save the small talk for the interview room!

Impressing In The Interview

1.   **'Practice, Practice, Practice!'** – There is a famous US Navy SEAL mantra that summarises this point perfectly:

> *"Under pressure, you don't rise to the occasion,*
> *you merely sink to the level of your training."*

People think that when they get to the interview, they will suddenly rise to the occasion, show the best version of themselves and respond brilliantly to everything they face in the interview room. In reality, they just sink to their level of training, and for most uni students, that training is non-existent. As a result, when the pressure kicks in, their mind goes blank, or they give a stupid answer that they kick themselves for later. Here are two ways you can train for the job interview and properly prepare yourself for the real thing:

A.   *Mock interviews* – Ask a family member or friend to do a mock interview with you. (If there is anyone you know who has experience with job interviews, or are in the field you are looking at going into, this will be incredibly useful.

However, practising with anyone is still beneficial.) After the mock interview, get them to give you honest, objective feedback on what you can improve on. Keep repeating until you become comfortable and you have taken on board all their feedback.

B. *Record yourself* – Have you ever heard your voice back on an audio recording and thought to yourself *"What on earth was that? Do I really sound like that?! That voice sounds completely different to the one I hear when I talk!"* The best way to find out about these blind spots is to video record yourself in a mock job interview. Whilst it can be cringe worthy watching it back, you will learn so much about yourself that you were never aware of. You may notice that you talk too fast, your voice is too monotone, you say 'err' too much, you ramble on, that your body language is very negative or that you don't make much eye contact. After watching yourself back, you will be mindful of these weaknesses and can improve on them before you get into a real job interview.

2. **Research The Interviewer** – If it is possible to find out who will be interviewing you, do some research on them beforehand. You can then use this knowledge when you meet this person to help create a bond between you and the interviewer, which will help you stand out amongst the other candidates. Try and find out information about their education, their skills, their background, their interests and their hobbies. Start by looking at their LinkedIn profile or any public social media accounts and see if there's any mutual ground. For example, let's say you're from the city they went to university in – try and subtly mention your hometown in the interview. Alternatively, if a search of their Twitter reveals they're a big techno head, when there's a bit of small talk before the interview or during the break, you could

bring up this topic of music. People tend to like other people who are similar to themselves, so showing that you have a shared interest with the interviewer will help to demonstrate this point and as a result, paint you in a more positive light. (Warning – avoid scrolling through their Facebook and accidentally liking one of their photos from their '2011 Trip to Ibiza' album!) Use a tool like Clearbit Connect, simply enter their email, and it will show you all their social media accounts.

3. **Get Out Of Your Head** – The majority of people go into a job interview thinking about what they want to get from the job. Do the opposite. Get out of your head and think about what the interviewer is looking for in a candidate. Think deeply about the questions they are likely to ask you, what these questions really mean and what answers they want to hear. When you get into the interview room, and they ask you a question, ask yourself before answering, '*Why have they asked me that question? What are they looking to find out about me by asking that question? Is there a hidden meaning behind it? What is the question behind the question?*'

    In your answers, try and avoid talking too much about yourself or the value the job will provide you. Instead, focus on them and the value you can provide. Rather than saying "*I would like a job that gives me responsibilities because I want...*" refocus on "*I believe I can provide value to you in X, Y, Z... I have experience in X from one of my university summers during which I did A, B and C*".

Uni Lifehacks: From 'A Secret Tool That Will Give You The CEO's Email Address', To 'The Best LinkedIn Tips & Tricks'

Become Bilingual – Learn a foreign language alongside your degree. You can use your university's free language classes, or you can use free tools such as Duolingo, which can help teach you the language you want to learn and track your progress. (You can now even add Duolingo to your Linkedin page as language proficiency.)

The British Council's *Languages For The Future Report* asked various companies to rate which languages were most useful to their organisation. (9). Here's the top ten:

1. French – 49%

2. German – 45%

3. Spanish – 34%

4. Polish – 29%

5. Mandarin Chinese – 28%

6. Arabic – 16%

7. Cantonese – 16%

8. Russian – 13%

9. Portuguese – 13%

10. Japanese – 8%

The Best Internship and Graduate Job Websites: *www.milkround .com, www.indeed.com, totaljobs.com, gradjobs.com, www.savethe graduate.org www.targetjobs.co.uk www.prospects.ac.uk www.intern wise.co.uk*

A Secret Tool That Will Give You The CEO's Email Address – Install a Google Chrome extension called 'Hunter'. Simply go to their website, press the Hunter button and it will give you a list of all the e-mail addresses associated with that organisation.

Lock Down Your Facebook Page – This is the oldest trick in the book. Your potential employers will almost certainly check out your Facebook page:

A. *Maximise your privacy settings* – Play around with Facebook's privacy settings to see what other people can see on your page.

B. *Remove any embarrassing public photos* – That funny photo of you on a sport social might not go down too well with future employers.

C. *Change your email address* – A lot of students change their names on Facebook so employers can't find them, however, the issue is that they also search for you via your email address too. So, if you really don't want them to find you, change the email address linked to your Facebook.

D. *Check all your other social media* – Don't just check Facebook, make sure your Twitter and Instagram don't have anything too embarrassing either.

The Best LinkedIn Tips And Tricks:

A. *Give out recommendations* – Ask your connections on LinkedIn to return the favour. You will then have a load of recommendations on your page.

B. *Join groups* – If you don't want to shell out on LinkedIn Premium but would like to contact someone who you are not connected with, join a group that they are part of. Once you are part of the group, you can message them.

C. Use the 'LinkedIn resume builder' – This will turn your LinkedIn profile into a professional looking CV in a PDF format.

Get To Know The Company Inside Out – If you are interested in working at a particular company or in a specific field, you can use Google alerts to keep up to date with all the news relating to that industry. This will keep you informed and make you appear more knowledgeable in the interview room.

The Ultimate Guide To Interview Prep: On The Day

A. *Workout* – Go for a workout on the day of the interview (or at least the day before). This will help with nerves and put you in a good mood. Exercise has been shown to reduce the body's level of cortisol, which is associated with feelings of stress. It has also been shown to increase your levels of serotonin, which is associated with positive moods (10).

B. *Power poses* – Change your body language beforehand. Research has shown that a simple two-minute change to your body language can positively impact interview performance. (See 'A 2 Minute Exercise Scientifically Proven To Make You Feel More Confident' on page 112)

C. *Make eye contact in the interview room* – It will make you more memorable, and will convey confidence, even if you don't feel it. A research study looked into the effects of eye contact. In the study, two groups were told to give a presentation. One group made no eye contact, while the other group made some eye contact. The participants who made some eye contact were reported to be 'significantly more likely to be remembered' than the participants who didn't. (Tip – If you find making eye contact difficult, focus on the point above their nose between their eyebrows, it will have the same effect.)

D. *Ask them questions* – You should ask the interviewer questions too, it shows them that you've thought about the interview beforehand and haven't just turned up on the day unprepared. It can also help by answering any questions you may have about the company and its practices, or how your application went:

- "How would I be expected to progress over the next five years?"

- "What would a typical work day look like?"

- "Was there anything about my interview or application that would mean I wouldn't be considered?"

- "What in my application qualified me for this role?"

- "Is my application missing anything?"

- "What about my application or interview can I improve upon?"

PART THREE

HEALTH

"You're like a completely new person. You look so much healthier since I last saw you three years ago! How much weight have you lost? Your skin looks amazing too, and you have so much energy during the day. What's your secret?"

"I went to university."

Let's be honest. This conversation has probably never happened. Most students leave university nowhere near as healthy as they were when they started. The student lifestyle isn't typically associated with a clean bill of health. However, it doesn't have to be that way. The seventh chapter of the book, *The Student Health & Fitness Guide*, will look at how you can keep your physical health in check while at university. It breaks down the three leading causes of student weight gain and the poor food choices which cause students problems, as well as a home gym you can build for just £50.

The next chapter, *Looking After Your Mind,* is based on a topic often neglected by students (and society in general for that matter), and as a result, it is one of the most important chapters in the book, if not the most important. Most people are taught about physical health from an early age, and they know roughly what to do lead a physically healthy lifestyle. For example, you probably know that to lose weight you should consume fewer calories than you burn, or that if you want to gain muscle you should lift weights, and you know if you have broken a leg you should probably go to the hospital. That is ingrained in us from an early age. The topic of mental health and mental well-being is rarely if ever, discussed. Think about it, can you remember someone ever teaching you about these topics at school? For the majority of us, there's never a conversation about how to deal with negative emotions or what professional services to reach out to if you are suffering from depression. University is a time where people need this information more than ever. This chapter provides mental health resources for contact if you are ever in need, as well as two scientifically proven techniques to make you feel less stressed and happier.

This part of the book finishes with Chapter Nine, providing you with vital information that will save you many a wasted day; in this chapter, we're going to tell you how to *Hack Your Hangover*. We take a look at the four main causes of a hangover, how many days the average student loses in bed hungover (it's a lot!) and the best hangover Lifehacks to get you feeling fresher and more productive the next day.

7

The Student Health & Fitness Guide

"Health is like money. We never have a
true idea of its value until we lose it."

– Josh Billings

"I am a firm believer in moderation in everything –
including moderation."

– Aubrey Marcus

The 3 Biggest Causes Of Student Weight Gain

Weight gain while at university is a well-documented phenomenon for students worldwide. A review of weight gain studies related to university students concluded that on average, 60% of university students gain weight in just their first year alone, with the average gain coming in at around 7.5lbs, nearly 3.5kg! (11)

Many students start their degree as fresh-faced, trim and toned, but leave with a severe case of 'dad bod'. Americans have their own term for it, 'The Freshman 15'. The '15' refers to the number of pounds some students put on in their first year of university (or 'college' if you're American.) So, why all the weight gain? No matter what stage of life you're at, weight gain can always be explained by viewing your body as an input-output system:

Inputs Vs Outputs

If your inputs (calories from food and drink) are greater than your outputs (calories burnt), you will gain weight. Alternatively, if your inputs are less than your outputs, then you will lose weight.

It's really that simple.

To put on one pound (lb) of body weight, you would need to eat 3,500 more calories than the energy your body burns. For example, if Tim's daily calorie maintenance (how many calories he needs to stay the same weight) is 2500 and he eats 3,000 calories every day for a week he will put on 1lb. This is because he has eaten 500 extra calories each day for seven days, which equates to the magic 3,500 calories. So if the average weight gain of students in their first year is 7.5 lbs, this means **they are consuming 26,250 calories MORE THAN their maintenance in just one year at university.**

Here are the three most common causes of weight gain at university (and their solutions!)

1. **Fast Food** – An online survey of over 10,000 university students found that on average, students spend £102.77 on takeaway food a month, which equates to an astounding £924.90 per academic year. The same survey also found that university students order takeaways an average of 8.3 times a month, compared to the 1.95 times a month for the wider UK population (12).

What's the problem? Other than the damage it does to your wallet, takeaways usually contain an extremely high number of calories. A single pot of Domino's Garlic and Herb Dip, the accompaniment that makes Domino's oh-so-good, contains 169 calories; and the big 100g pot contains 675 calories, so be wary. Below are the calorie breakdowns of some popular student takeaway choices, and some healthier alternatives:

Food	Calories (kcal)	Replace With	Calories (kcal)
Domino's Medium Classic Crust Original Cheese & Tomato Pizza	1160	Domino's Medium Thin Crust Original Low Fat Cheese & Tomato Pizza	848
Chicken Legend with Cool Mayo And Medium Fries	866	BBQ Chicken BLC and Medium Fries	659
Zinger Tower Burger	620	Toasted Twister Wrap	480
Wetherspoons Large Breakfast	1629	Wetherspoons Traditional Breakfast	961
Burger King Double Whopper Sandwich With Medium Fries	1120	Burger King Angus Classic With Medium Fries	860
Ben and Jerry's 500ml Cookie Dough Tub	1150	Oppo Colombian Chocolate and Hazelnut 500ml Tub	420

2. **Alcohol** – If you like a drink, this can be one of the biggest causes of weight gain at uni. Alcoholic drinks vary, but many of them are packed with calories. Not only that, alcohol is very similar to fizzy drinks, in that it doesn't fill you up. These 'empty' calories have the opposite effect – they make you hungrier, particularly

for fast foods! That greasy meal will seem even more appealing after a few drinks. A study on mice found that after a few drinks (not literally, they were given an ethanol-water solution by scientists), they ate 10-25% more than they usually would eat. A brain scan of the tipsy mice showed that alcohol activated specific parts of the brain associated with the urge to eat (13). Stopping drinking altogether is not the only option however, by just swapping drinks for lower calorie alternatives, you can cut a big chunk out of your calorie intake.[10]

Drink*	Serving Size	Calories (Kcal)	Replace With	Serving Size	Calories (Kcal)
Carlsberg (2.2 units)	568ml (1 pint)	182	Bacardi and Diet Coke (1.9 units)	50ml (with 250ml Diet Coke)	104
Strongbow (2.8 units)	568ml (1 pint)	200	Smirnoff Vodka and Zero Sugar Squash (1.9 units)	50ml (with 250ml Squash)	106
Blossom Hill White Wine (1.5 units)	125ml (1 small glass)	95	Southern Comfort and Diet Lemonade (1 unit)	25ml (with 250ml Diet Lemonade)	56
Guinness (2.3 units)	568ml (1 pint)	210	Jack Daniels and Diet Pepsi (2 units)	50ml (with 250ml Diet Pepsi)	112

Drink*	Serving Size	Calories (Kcal)	Replace With	Serving Size	Calories (Kcal)
WKD (1.1 unit)	275ml	182	Gordons Gin and Diet Tonic (0.9 units)	25ml (1 shot)	53
Jägerbomb (1 unit)	25ml (with 250ml Redbull)	210	Sambuca (1 unit)	25ml (1 shot)	90

The Maths Of Switching Drinks At Uni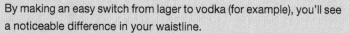

By making an easy switch from lager to vodka (for example), you'll see a noticeable difference in your waistline.

If you drink on average ten units per night[10], that equates to 827 calories if you drink lager, and 557 calories if you drink vodka. That's a difference of 270 calories per night! If you go out 1-3 times per week over 3x12-week terms, here's how the maths will add up across your time at uni:

270-810 calories per week
3,240-9,720 calories per term
9,720-29,160 calories per year
29,160-87,480 calories across your time at university.

These numbers might seem crazy, but hear us out. To put them into perspective, if it takes a 3,500 caloric surplus to put on a lb of body weight, (and if we assume that in the vodka example you are hitting your caloric maintenance for the day) **this could prevent 8-24lbs of weight gain across your time at uni!**

---

[10] Disclaimer – PLEASE DRINK RESPONSIBLY!! The UK Chief Medical Officers recommend that men and women do not consume over 14 units per week. We know that some university students have the tendency to drink far beyond that; and the last thing we want to do is encourage binge drinking, so please moderate your drinking habits and visit *www.drinkaware.co.uk* for more information.

3. **Sugary Drinks** – If you drink a one-litre bottle of Coca-Cola as your Netflix companion, you are putting 108g of carbohydrates, or 420 calories, into your body. The most troubling thing about these calories is that they are often referred to as 'empty calories' because they don't fill you up in the same way that food does. This means that you will still be hungry after drinking it and may end up consuming even more calories from food. Fizzy drinks aren't the only culprits, a lot of smoothies and juice drinks have as much sugar and calories, and in some cases, more! (There's no need for a comparison table on this one, it's so simple – just drink the diet alternative, or even better, water.)

How To Apply This At University – Staying Lean And Avoiding 'The Freshman 15'

1. **JOIN a sports team** – Exercise is always more fun when it's with your mates doing a sport you enjoy. The regular training sessions and matches will help you burn through your fair share of calories. The routine and structure will likely help with your diet too – it's hard to justify that Big Mac when you have a game later that afternoon.

2. **Get a GYM-BUDDY** – It's much more difficult to skip a workout when your training partner has set off to meet you at the gym. Not only will they hold you accountable for turning up to workout, but they will also push you and motivate you throughout your workout. (Make sure you pick someone who is reliable and motivated to improve!)

3. **Book a SUMMER HOLIDAY** – When you have an end goal in sight, it's very easy to get yourself motivated to exercise and stay healthy. Whenever it comes times to work out or cook a healthy meal, the thought of you lying on a beach will be present in the back of your mind and help to keep you on track.

How To Build A Home Gym For Just £50

Gym memberships are without a doubt hugely beneficial to keeping your health in check at uni. However, a home gym can be just as important. A problem I had at uni was that whenever my schedule was hectic, or I was hungover and couldn't be bothered travelling to the gym, I would just skip a workout. Over time, the workouts I missed added up to ten to twenty over an entire term; and I found that whenever I missed workouts, it became a lot easier to justify eating junk food too. It's a negative cycle that feeds on itself (or in my case, on Mr Kipling's Angel Cakes). So, I put together a home gym that I could use whenever I couldn't be bothered or didn't have the time to trek to the gym. It's hard to make excuses when you have a gym a couple of feet away from your bed. On the next page are some key items for home-workout success:

The Student £50 Home Gym

1. **Pull Up Bar** – All you need is a door frame to attach it to. You can do wide grip, narrow grip and chin ups on this bar. If you are currently not strong enough to do pull-ups just put a chair underneath you and use it to take some of the weight. (Alternatively, try some 'doorway rows', which you can do for free by using your bodyweight and the door frame to build up strength.) The bar also enables you to do various ab exercises such as crunches or leg raises.

    Price – £10

2. **Weight Set** – Just £20 will get you 20KG worth of dumbbells, enabling you to work various muscles in any way you can think of: from squats and lunges to bicep curls and shoulder presses. If you need more than 10KG for each dumbbell, use

one dumbbell at a time, and work your right side and then your left side (or vice versa), this will enable you to get up to 20KG on one dumbbell. Another weight alternative is kettlebells, these can be used just like dumbbells, but they also allow an entirely different style of workout. (For a tough but super simple workout, try 'Kettlebells: Simple and Sinister' by Pavel Tsatsouline!)

Price – £20

3. **Resistance Bands** – This is the most versatile item on the list. They work off the resistance you apply and give you the ability to do so many different exercises, working every muscle in your body.

Price – £10

4. **Uni Rucksack** – This DIY technique will without a doubt add a little extra intensity to your workouts. Any mild exercise or activity you do, you can now add additional weight to. Fill a rucksack with your heaviest reading materials or the dumbbell set from above, and lo-and-behold, you have given your workout a whole new dimension. If you do bodyweight squats and find it easy, try it with the weighted backpack on instead.

Similarly, if you find regular press-ups a piece of cake, then try adding this extra weight to really challenge yourself. (For advanced lifters who need more than a weighted rucksack to break a sweat, try adding exercises like pistol squats or pike pulses to your home workout routine.)

Price – Free

5. **Household Equipment** – If you have two chairs that are of similar height, you can use them to do dips and ab raises. You can use a single chair to do decline push ups or box squats. Alternatively, think outside the box and get creative; it will depend on your living situation, but I used two equally balanced kitchen work surfaces to do dips on. (If you are a

more advanced lifter looking for a real challenge, try handstand press-ups. They will be near enough impossible at first, but they'll have an enormous impact on your physical capabilities if you keep trying them.)

Price – Free

6. **Foam Roller** – This can come in handy when it comes to warming up or rehabbing any stiff areas of the body. Unlike stretching, it lets you target specific areas of tightness. Foam rolling is a preventive action that is going to reduce your chances of an injury later down the line as well as improve your flexibility and mobility. When you spend all day at your desk typing an essay or writing an exam, getting on the foam roller can do wonders for your posture and how you generally feel. (If you are looking to take it to the next level, get a lacrosse ball.)

Price – £10

7. **Virtual Personal Trainer** – You can get a personal trainer to join you in your home gym. There's so many experts on YouTube as well as a load of free apps (see page 76) that guide you through whatever workout you choose to do.

Price – Free

Uni Lifehacks: From 'How To Get Rid Of Pesky Spots In Just 48 Hours' To 'The Smoothest Shave Of Your Life'

How To Get Rid Of Pesky Spots In Just 48 hours – Having a high-end beautician for an aunt isn't something we're all fortunate enough to have. However, David does, and she let him in on one of the best spot removers of all time… Surgical spirit. You can pick it up from any pharmacy; just dab the tip of a cotton bud dipped in spirit onto the offending spot and let it dry. After a day or two, your spot will have dried out and should be completely gone.

No-Nonsense Supplements For The Student Lifestyle:

A. *Multivitamin* – This can be particularly useful if you are on a tight budget, as the majority of students are, as you can increase the vitamins and minerals in your diet without having to spend money on expensive food.

B. *Vitamin D* – The primary source of vitamin D is the sun. Therefore, living in the UK means that you don't get it very often. This is particularly true at university as you are there for the least sunny seasons of the year – the autumn, winter and spring. Inadequate levels of vitamin D have been associated with feelings of depression and fatigue. (14)

C. *ZMA (Zinc, Magnesium, and Vitamin B6)* – The most common cause of insufficient magnesium and zinc is poor diet, sweat, and excessive alcohol consumption. As a student, your diet isn't always up to scratch on such a small budget. Your sweat and alcohol levels tend to be higher than the average person's, especially after a night out where you spent many hours on the packed dance floor, and you've had one Jägerbomb too many. Inadequate zinc and magnesium levels have been associated with increased feelings of lethargy, reduced sleep quality and skin breakouts. (15) (16)

D. *Fish oil (omega-3)* – A recent study found that university students who took fish oil reported a 20% reduction in their levels of anxiety during their studies in comparison to the placebo group. The body cannot produce omega-3 naturally, so it's very beneficial to consume fish oil, whether through fish itself (such as salmon or tuna) or by taking a fish oil supplement (17).

E. *5-HTP* – People who take 5-HTP often report decreases in negative feelings like depression and anxiety. Multiple trials have shown increased sleep quality with supplementation, and 5-HTP has been clinically proven to increase serotonin levels (one of the neurotransmitters our brain produces to affect how happy or anxious we feel). It can be a useful supplement during a stressful exam period or when you are looking to recover from a few late night outs, as people with increased levels of serotonin are reported to experience increased levels of relaxation and sociability (18).

The Smoothest Shave Of Your Life – If you find that your skin is being irritated by shaving foam, just use hair conditioner. It's the smoothest shave you'll have, it's designed to soften hair, and it'll probably save you a bit of cash too.

6 Apps That Will Help You Keep On Top Of Your Physical Health At Uni – Due to the cocktail of stress and various forms of temptation at university (as well as actual cocktails), it can be quite difficult to maintain a clean bill of physical health throughout term time. So you should use every bit of technology out there to support your physical health, and set yourself up for success in this area:

A. *Freeletics* – It has a huge variety of workouts that you can do at home, and it takes into consideration your fitness levels so you will find a workout tailored for you.

B. *Spotify Running* – This gauges the pace you are running at and will play corresponding songs from your library (or theirs) matching song tempo to your running speed. When you're about to start your final hill sprint, the last thing you want is your shuffle to change the song to your classical music studying playlist.

C. *Global Yoga Academy* – If you don't fancy turning up to your university yoga class for the first time and having to do the downward dog in front of someone from your seminar, download this and perfect your yoga moves at home. The app has loads of video instructions with narration that you can do in the comforts of your own bedroom. It has customised workouts that take into consideration how flexible you are and even enables you to schedule it into your calendar. The perfect way to unwind and take a break during a heavy academic period. (Alternative apps include Down Dog, 5 Minute Yoga and YogaGlo)

D. *Fitness Buddy* – This has over 400 exercises with 'detailed descriptions, animations and assortment of workouts'. A way to learn a tonne of new exercises and master the correct form without having to shell out half your student loan on personal trainer fees.

E. *MyFitnessPal* – Simply scan the barcode of the foods you have eaten, or search it by name and add it to your daily calorie consumption diary. You can then get a breakdown of how many calories you consumed that day, which sources you got them from (carbohydrates, fats and proteins) and set measurable goals for yourself. A recent study at Glasgow University saw a 50% reduction in weight gain when students were aware of the calories in the food they were consuming! (19)

F. *Strava* – 'Get key stats like distance, pace, speed, elevation gained and calories burned, as well as an interactive map' of your run or cycle. Also, if you have a regular route you take, you can compare your performance with previous attempts and track personal bests.

Staying On Top Of Your Sexual Health

A. *Get free protection* – You can save a lot of money as well as awkward conversations in shops by getting your protection from a sexual health clinic or a GP's surgery.

You can kill two birds with one stone by getting a sexual health check up while you are there.

B. *Set yourself up for success* – The majority of people would never eat a greasy kebab when they are sober and aren't hungry. However, when they are intoxicated and peckish, it's a different story. Lots of students would never consider having unprotected sex when they are sober and thinking rationally either. But when you add alcohol and hormones to the mix, you may make decisions you never would have imagined. A common piece of advice is, 'If you want to increase your chances of going to the gym, pack your bag the night before, it'll be one less thing to worry about'. Using that same logic, always carry protection in your wallet or purse. If an unanticipated occasion arises, you'll be prepared and won't have to rely on willpower to say no. Nothing kills the moment like having to run down to the local Co-op to get some protection.

8

Looking After Your Mind

"I think the saddest people always try their
hardest to make people happy because they
know what it's like to feel absolutely worthless
and don't want anyone else to feel like that."

–ROBIN WILLIAMS

"Oh yes, the past can hurt. But from the way I see it,
you can either run from it, or learn from it."

–RAFIKI, LION KING

Before we begin, for the purposes of this book, we have
made a clear distinction between mental health and mental
well-being. The term 'mental health' here will refer to any serious
medical conditions that you have been diagnosed with or believe
yourself to suffer from. The term 'mental well-being' will refer to any
negative emotions, feelings, or mindsets that you may be experiencing at university and that you can try to overcome through the
use of certain exercises and changes in perspective. To further

illustrate the differences between the two: mental health concerns students who are suffering from illnesses such as clinical depression or an anxiety disorder, mental well-being concerns students who are feeling emotions like sadness or stress, for example. It goes without saying that this is not an official distinction or terminology, and it is not black or white for everyone either. That said, it is still worth making the distinction. That is not to say that the exercises and perspectives in the mental well-being section of the book will not necessarily benefit people who suffer from mental health conditions. The purpose of this foreword is to make it clear that this is not professional medical advice. It is also to clarify that mental illness is in no way made light of by assuming that exercises and perspectives can in any way 'cure' a mental illness.

Mental Health Support Contacts If You Are Ever In Need

If you believe that you have a mental health problem, try and talk to someone about it, because you are not alone. Loved ones like family and friends are a great starting point, and you should also try and speak to a GP and get a medical consultation.

If you know friends that are suffering from mental health problems, do your best to listen and be there for them.

Your university will have some form of mental health support that you'll be able to contact as well as support staff, such as welfare officers on hand and a counselling service. These people are trained professionals, who are used to helping students struggling with mental health issues and can be a great source of help, advice, and support. There are also a whole host of great organisations out there offering you support during your time at university if you are ever struggling with mental health issues. To name just a few:

1. **Mind** – *www.mind.org.uk* – A UK mental health charity that offers support. 'We're here to make sure no one has to face a mental health problem alone'.

2. **Nightline** – *www.nightline.ac.uk* – Confidential, anonymous, non-judgmental, non-directive and non-advisory listening support service. Nightline is a service provided for students for the duration of their studies. It covers over 90 universities and colleges in the UK and Ireland.

3. **Student Minds** – *www.studentminds.org.uk* – 'The UK's Student Mental Health Charity'. Student Minds provides support groups and offers various resources related to mental health issues you or a friend may be facing.

4. **Mental Health Foundation** – *www.mentalhealth.org.uk* 'Support and Research for good mental health'. The Mental Health Foundation offers various forms of support and looks at cutting-edge research in the field of mental health.

5. **Samaritans** – *www.samaritans.org* – A confidential, voluntary phone line and support system that is open 24-7 which enables to talk to someone or seek support.

Here are two apps that may prove to be useful too:

1. **7 Cups** – There are a lot of university students who struggle to talk about the issues that they may be dealing with. This is a free app that provides an anonymous, confidential messenger service with trained volunteers who will listen to your problems. The app also suggests various skills you can learn to help deal with any issues that you may be facing.

2. **Stay Alive** – Stay Alive is a 'pocket suicide prevention resource' for people who are experiencing suicidal thoughts or are concerned

about someone else who may be. It provides numerous contact resources, a safety plan, a list of reasons for living and a life box to store photos that you cherish.

Your Mental Well-Being

University is an emotional rollercoaster at the best of times. It marks your first time living away from home and experiencing the first glimmer of independence: managing your finances, diet, deadlines, and trying to balance socialising alongside all of these things. (Not to mention that many students are consuming a depressant – alcohol – on a regular basis, and are often sleep deprived!) All of these factors mean that there are probably going to be a few tough days, or even weeks, at university, regardless of how positive and resilient you consider yourself to be. Just ask any graduate. In the next two passages, we have outlined two scientifically backed techniques we discovered that helped with our mental well-being during difficult periods at university.

How To Reduce Your Stress With This Ancient Technique

What do all the following people have in common?

- Beyonce – 17 million albums sold and twenty-two time Grammy Award winner
- Lionel Messi – Five-time Ballon D'or Winner
- Ariana Huffington – President and Editor-in-Chief, Huffington Post

- Mark Zuckerberg – Founder and CEO, Facebook
- Conor McGregor – The first fighter in UFC history to hold two titles in two weight divisions simultaneously
- Oprah Winfrey – Host of the highest-rated talk show in American history
- LeBron James – Three-time NBA finalist and three-time NBA Final MVP winner
- Serena Williams – 39 Total Gram Slam titles
- Ray Dalio – Manager, Bridgewater Associates (the world's largest hedge fund)
- Richard Branson – Serial Entrepreneur and Founder of Virgin

They all practice some form of meditation.

If practising meditation can improve the lives of some of the world's most successful entrepreneurs who are running businesses on the global stage, or help world class athletes perform to the best of their abilities in front of millions of people, then it can probably help you too. Also, if those people can find time to do it, anyone can.

After all, everyone has the exact same amount of hours in their day.

What is meditation? Before experiencing or reading about meditation, people tend to think of the following stereotype: sitting with legs crossed, barefooted, humming, chasing a state of 'thoughtlessness', and saying "*namaste*" when finished. I used to think this, and I also had a four letter expletive for people who did it too! The stereotype simply isn't true. There are so many different ways to meditate. It's practised by millions of individuals across the globe, not just by celibate monks halfway up a mountain.

The Monkey Mind

One great analogy to keep in mind when thinking about meditation is that your mind is full of excitable and 'drunken' monkeys. These monkeys are the thoughts and emotions we have that are screeching, chattering and crashing cymbals in our heads, constantly distracting us. We all have 'monkey minds', and we may have dozens of monkeys (the constant thoughts and worries in our head), all wanting to be heard and given our full attention. By meditating, these loud, chattering monkeys are tameable, and over time you can learn to control them. Fighting the monkeys is futile, because as the saying goes, *that which you resist, persists*. Taming the monkeys can be achieved by spending a small amount of time each day calming the mind through simple breathing exercises; no need for uncomfortable positions or bizarre humming sounds.

You may still be sceptical, but just look at the research:

1. **Reduces Stress** – A study at Stanford University found that a meditation course reduced reactivity in the part of the brain associated with fear (the amygdala). It also found that participants had decreased levels of stress due to increased activity in the prefrontal cortex, the region of the brain which helps regulate our emotions (20).

2. **Increases Focus And Willpower** – Another study examined how meditation training affected individuals' behaviour in multitasking at work. The researchers concluded that, in comparison with the people who didn't meditate, *"those trained in meditation stayed on tasks longer and made fewer switches, as well as reporting less negative feedback after performing the task."* (21)

3. **Increases Emotional Control** – In a study at Michigan State University, participants who had never practised meditation

were split into two groups. One group practised meditation for the first time while the other group were kept busy with another task. Afterwards, both groups were shown some emotionally 'disturbing pictures'. When analysing the brains of both groups, the research showed that the group who practised meditation had greater emotional control and could recover to a neutral state faster than the group who didn't meditate (22) (23).

There will be many situations where you'll feel stressed and anxious; deadlines, first dates and job interviews could all be contributing factors. Regular practice of meditation will help with this and will be useful at university and beyond.

There are many different ways to meditate, but a great beginner's technique is to focus on your breathing for a set period of time. A common assumption that people make is that the aim of meditation is to completely clear your head of any thoughts. Individuals with this misconception get frustrated with themselves and the whole concept of meditation. This can lead to people giving up on it and thinking it is a pointless exercise. The aim of meditation is **not** to achieve a state of thoughtlessness, this state is rarely attained by Buddhist monks who have been practising every day for decades.

How To Apply This At University – Clearing Your Mind

1. **FOCUS on your breathing** – This is surprisingly difficult to do; your focus will inevitably wander. You will catch yourself lost in thought, whether it's what you are going to make for dinner that night, the guy who constantly sniffs in your seminar or the guy or girl you flirt with in the library cafe. You'll then get annoyed at

yourself for losing your focus. This is proceeded by you getting more annoyed at yourself for getting annoyed at yourself, all while drifting further off task. **The aim is not to clear your head of thoughts. The aim is to bring your focus back to your breathing whenever you find yourself lost in your thoughts.** See it as a mental workout. Every time you bring your attention back to your breathing, you'll have completed a 'mental rep'. Like any exercise in the gym, with each rep, you will become stronger, and in this case, better at keeping your focus.

2. **Start with 5 MINUTES every day** – Sit down for five minutes at the beginning and/or end of your day. Throughout the five minutes, try and focus solely on your breathing. Whenever you catch your attention drifting off into a chain of thoughts (and you will), try to observe the thoughts without judgement and then bring your focus back to your breathing. With time, you can increase the length of the sessions, but start small and instead concentrate on making a habit of it. Be patient – it usually takes seven to fourteen days before you start noticing any differences in your everyday mental state. (Try an app like Headspace or Calm, both of which offer free introductory sessions on meditation. The best guided meditation I have used is 'Sam Harris – Guided Meditation' on YouTube. There's a short version and a long version available.)

How to Feel Happier Through Use of A Simple Daily Practice

You have probably had a day similar to this: you're super stressed out because life has decided to throw everything at you from the minute you woke up. You might be having relationship drama, an argument with your parents, looming deadlines, or any number of other problems. You sit and wonder '*why me?*'

As you are wallowing in your own misery and self-pity, something happens that puts everything into perspective. You hear of someone losing a loved one; see a charitable appeal for people barely surviving in the third world; walk past someone in the street who is blind, or is missing something that you take for granted every single day. All of a sudden your life isn't quite as bad as you thought it was. Your self-pity and anger fade away. **You feel a real-life high on the <u>gratitude</u> for what you have.** Ultimately, if you're even reading this, you are *incredibly* lucky. You won the quality of life lottery. The odds of the quality of your existence are unfathomable. Firstly, of the 8.7 million species known to man, you were born human, the most intelligent life form on the planet. Secondly, of the 300 million sperm cells you were competing against, you won the race. Thirdly, out of all the possible time in human history, you were born now, in an era in which you never have to worry about fighting in the trenches of a World War or catching smallpox. And finally, out of all the locations on Earth, you were born in the UK (or can afford to go to university here), which means you are financially better off than 95% of the world. As you were fortunate enough to be born on this particular island (or continent for that matter) you never have to worry about the cleanliness of your drinking water or worry about where your next meal is going to come from.

You won the most ridiculous lottery of all time.
To put it simply: Life is good.

Despite this, you will probably find yourself getting stressed about what you think at the time are serious problems. Maybe you didn't get the grade you wanted, someone isn't texting you back, or you got rejected from the graduate scheme that you applied for. Of course, getting stressed by these things is entirely natural, and they are sometimes a great source of motivation to work harder or to do things differently next time. However, it's important to keep your problems in perspective, and not to let them ruin what could otherwise be a great day or week. Remember: you are in the physical prime of your life, with no real responsibilities and you're getting a degree, there's a lot to be happy about. Appreciating and being thankful for the things that are good in your life is called 'gratitude'. Again, if you are a sceptic like myself, you may think appreciating the things you have and being grateful is a load of new age nonsense, but again just look at the research:

1. **Improved Mood** – Dr Emmons, Professor of Psychology and the world's leading expert on gratitude, has produced various studies that show a positive correlation between levels of gratitude and happiness. One study revealed that a group who regularly engaged in gratitude were 'more empathetic, forgiving, helpful and supportive' compared to the group who did not regularly engage in gratitude exercises. The study also found that the group who frequently expressed gratitude experienced 'more positive emotions' than the group that did not. According to Emmons, the practice of gratitude trained their 'prefrontal cortex to retain more positive information and spend less time focusing on negative information' (24).

2. **Improved Mental Strength** – One study found that Vietnam War veterans who had higher levels of gratitude experienced 'lower rates of PTSD' in comparison to the group who had lower levels of gratitude (25). Furthermore, another study found that a significant contributor to the mental resilience of people after the World Trade Centre attacks was gratitude (26).

3. **Improved Relationship Quality** – A recent study into the effects of gratitude on relationships found that 'feelings of gratitude were the most consistent predictor of relationship quality (as well as the likelihood of the couple remaining together!) Gratitude also benefits friendships too. A study published in

the *Journal of Happiness Studies* found that those who practised gratitude towards people they met developed more friendships as well as forming higher quality connections (27).

Again, at university, your mood isn't always going to be perfect; there will be days when you wake up on the wrong side of the bed. Practising gratitude regularly will positively impact your mental state throughout your time at uni.

How To Apply This To University – Keeping An Attitude Of Gratitude

1. **Think of three things you are GRATEFUL for –** Do this every morning (or at least on the mornings where you feel like rubbish). One by one, take each of the things you are grateful for and write them down. Try and think of new things each day.

2. **Don't take anything for GRANTED –** This is an ancient technique from the Stoic philosopher Seneca called 'Negative Visualisation'. The technique asks you to take an awful situation, like losing a loved one, losing your eyesight, becoming seriously ill, or any other potentially harrowing situation that you're fortunate enough not to have actually happened to you, **and truly visualise what it would be like if it did happen.** At first, the feelings will be terrifying; but in the same way you feel the immense relief of waking up after a nightmare and realising that it was all a dream, you'll feel intense relief and gratitude for not really being in that situation. Seneca said 'all we have is on loan from fortune' and as such, fortune can take it back whenever it wants. When you repeatedly take on the mindset of negative visualisation, it's the ultimate happiness hack, as it makes you desire what you already have (28).

Uni Lifehacks: From 'Getting An Amazing Night's Sleep In Student Accommodation' To 'A Tool That Will Give You Unlimited Willpower'

Getting An Amazing Night's Sleep In Student Accommodation:

A. *Get some silicone ear plugs* – If you don't have these on hand, you will wish you did when you have an exam the next day and there's a party starting across the road, or if your flatmate is deathly allergic to having quiet sex. The silicone enables you to mould the earplug to fit your ear perfectly, so it is more comfortable, less likely to fall out, and reduces the external sound most effectively.

B. *Get an eye mask* – When the light seeps through your window in the early hours, this can come in handy. You can also take it to the next level and get a lavender scented eye mask. According to the National Sleep Foundation, participants who smelt lavender before bed had a deeper sleep and felt more energised in the morning.

C. *Download F.Lux* – When you look at a screen before bed, the 'blue light' emitted from your screen suppresses your body's melatonin production, a chemical your body produces to regulate your sleeping pattern. F.Lux adjusts your computer screen late at night to a redder light, which doesn't affect your melatonin production. (It's a feature called Night Shift on iPhones and Macs, or an app called Twilight on Google Play.)

D. *Get a mattress topper* – This is a ridiculously soft mini-mattress that just sits on top of the ordinary mattress, making your bed softer and your sleep better. The average person spends a reported third of their life in bed, with the average student probably nearer to two-thirds of their time at university in bed! This is a smart investment that your future self will thank you for every single day.

E. *Download Sleep Cycle* – Throughout the night you go through sleep cycles (of light sleep to deep sleep) around every 90 minutes. No matter how long you have slept for, if you wake up in a deep sleep, you will feel like death. Sleep Cycle wakes you up when you are at the lightest stage of your sleep, within a specific window dependent on which time you set your alarm for. No more bleary-eyed 9 AM lectures.

F. *Download Relax Melodies* – If you don't have the silicone earplugs on hand, or you just want something to tone down the noise from the flat party next-door – try Relax Melodies. You can create your own mix and sleep to over 50 relaxing sounds including white noise, binaural beats and soothing melodies.

The Power Of Walking – Whenever you are feeling stressed out or overworked, put on your favourite playlist or podcast and go for a walk. Why?

A. *Mood* – A study of university students found that students who spent just twelve minutes walking experienced increased self-confidence, motivation and joy in comparison to the group of students who spent their time sat down (29).

B. *Essay creativity* – Research performed by Stanford University found that walkers produced 'two times the amount of creative responses' than people who were sat down (30).

C. *Freshers flu* – A study by the British Journal of Sports Medicine found that participants who walked twenty minutes a day for 5 days a week were 43% less likely to get sick than people who didn't.

D. *Junk food cravings* – Researchers at the University of Exeter found that fifteen-minute walks can reduce snacking on junk food by up to 50% (31).

A Tool That Will Give You Unlimited Willpower – It takes an estimated twenty-one days to form a new habit, and consistently implementing positive behaviour for that long requires a tonne of willpower. Whether it's sticking to a new diet, making your 9 AM lectures or giving up smoking – it can be hard to make a change. StickK plays on loss aversion, the idea that the human brain is more motivated by avoiding losses than it is by acquiring gains. (People are more motivated by the thought of losing £10 than they are by gaining £10.) **Some studies have observed that the brain reacts to a loss twice as much as it does an equivalent gain** (32)**.** StickK allows you to use this to your advantage by hacking your willpower. You just state what target you want to achieve that week and how much money it should take out of your account if you don't achieve it. i.e. if you don't go to the gym five times that week, you have to give away £10. StickK lets you take this one step further by choosing a friend as the receiver of money, and when those sort of stakes are on the line, you'll definitely achieve your goals. (If that's not enough, you can choose an anti-charity such as a political party whose views you strongly disagree with.)

An Instant Mood Change – Whenever you wake up on the wrong side of the bed, or you are stressing about the future, put your headphones in and listen to *Everybody's Free To Wear Sunscreen* by Baz Luhrmann.

How To Break Free Of Social Media Addiction – The research varies, but it's been estimated that the average young person spends anywhere between 1 hour and 40 minutes to 9 hours per day on social media! Social media has been designed to be as addictive as possible – it produces a spike of the reward chemical dopamine in our brain. One way to get out of its addictive grasp is simple yet so effective; log out of your accounts. When you have to manually type in your login details, this acts as an obstacle to your autopilot social media surfing. (I found this little hack cut my social media usage from 10-20 times daily to 1-2 times a day.)

How To Get Yourself Out Of A Slump – At university, it's natural to go through ups and downs. You may be going through a break-up, questioning what you want to do with your life or be at your most stressed with deadlines or exams. During these slumps, there may be dark days, where you're alone in your room with your thoughts and nothing seems to be going your way; and no amount of gratitude or meditation is going to get you out of it. We've been there too. Here's a collection of advice from a variety of people who have battled and overcome slumps in their lives:

A. *Get out of bed* – This can be really hard, especially during the times when you're in a negative state of mind. However, do your best to get out of bed as soon as you wake up. Staying in bed will only make you feel worse.

B. *Hygiene >* – It's amazing what a warm shower, brushing your teeth and putting on some nice, clean clothes can do for your mental state. Get freshened up and you'll immediately feel better.

C. *Do something physical* – Various studies have shown exercise to be as effective as antidepressants. Whether it's a light stroll down to the supermarket and back or a 5K run, just try and get active.

D. *Schedule negativity* – One of the most effective methods for losing weight is the counterintuitive 'cheat meal'. When people have a cheat meal scheduled in, they find it much easier to stay on track with their nutrition throughout the week, as they know when they will soon be indulging in their craving.

Try doing the same with your negative emotions – schedule in when you allow yourself to feel negative. Take the break-up example. Instead of spending every minute of each day fighting the pain that you are feeling about being dumped and ultimately cracking numerous times throughout the day, schedule in a period of time where you can be absolutely miserable about it. (E.g. 'I can lie in bed upset about missing them between 5 PM and 5:30 PM'.) During that time, feel free to curl in a ball under your duvet, eat as much Ben & Jerry's as you see fit and listen to the top five most played Dido songs on Spotify. However, as soon as the allotted time period is up, you're not allowed to think negatively about that situation up until 5 PM the next day. This technique is incredibly effective, as you don't have to spend your day trying to forever resist negative emotions; you only have to wait until 5 PM! The trick is to reduce the frequency of these periods as time goes on until you no longer feel the need to schedule in the time slot.

E. *Use momentum* – Psychological momentum is often described as being 'on a roll' or 'a winning streak'. It's so powerful that 92% of sports coaches believe that performance is crucially determined by momentum (33). Look at the list of tasks that you have to do that day, and identify the easiest task and the most important one. Do the easiest one first to build some momentum, then do the most important task next. Once the first task is done, the second one you do – the most important – will be far easier to get on with.

Hack Your Hangover

"I never met anyone who gets up out of their bed after a night on the town and says, 'Oh I wish I'd had another drink last night. That would have been a great idea.'"

–Arthur Matthews

"The only real cure for a hangover is death."

–Robert Benchley

The Four Main Causes of A Hangover

The effects of a hangover vary from person to person, and science hasn't quite figured out what exactly it is about drinking alcohol that causes hangovers and the individual differences that people experience. Science has, however, given us some insight into what factors are most likely to cause hangovers:

1. **Dehydration** – Alcohol is a diuretic, meaning it reduces the levels of a hormone called vasopressin, which is responsible for making your kidneys reabsorb water rather than releasing it as

urine. Reduced levels of vasopressin result in dehydration, as your body urinates the water rather than retaining it.

2. **Vitamin and Mineral Depletion** – Your body's vitamin and mineral levels take a serious hit when you drink a lot of alcohol. These vitamins and minerals are needed for the body to function normally, hence you don't feel normal the next day!

3. **Acetaldehyde Build Up** – When alcohol passes through your liver, it gets converted into a harmful toxin (acetaldehyde). High levels of this toxin are associated with cognitive impairment, memory loss, dry mouth and tiredness (A.K.A the usual hangover symptoms). Your liver naturally produces a potent detoxifying agent (glutathione) that helps get rid of the toxin from your system. This is why how much you drink is usually correlated with how bad you feel the next day. The more of the toxin you have in your system, the longer it takes for your body to produce the amount of detoxifying agent needed.

4. **Lack Of Sleep Or Low-Quality Sleep** – Regardless of whether or not you drank the night before, if you get in at 4 AM and you have to be up at 9 AM for a lecture, you're never going to feel completely fresh. However, if you did drink, the quality of your sleep is also going to be affected. During the night, you usually have between five and six cycles of REM sleep (the deepest possible sleep cycle), which leaves you feeling refreshed. However, if you've been drinking, you'll typically only have one or two cycles, meaning your body wakes up feeling like you have had a full night's sleep, however, come mid-afternoon, you feel exhausted.

How Many Days The Average Uni Student Spends Hungover

Hangovers can lead to you spending all day in bed, feeling ill, and overeating. This behaviour is not conducive to a positive, healthy, or fulfilled uni experience. If you lie in bed doing nothing except feeling sorry for yourself after every night out, the days will add up.

The Maths Of The Student Hangover

Let's say that the average student goes out drinking 1-3 times per week and studies for three years. If you have 3 x 12-week terms then it adds up to the following:

- **12-36 days per term** lying in bed hungover.
- **36-108 days per year** lying in bed hungover.
- **108-324 uni days in total spent lying in bed hungover.**

If you are on a three-year course, you will only have 756 days at university, which means that if you don't learn how to conquer the next day and get things done even after a night out, you can end up spending between **14%-42% of your time at university lying in bed hungover.**

I had some personal experience with this at university. After a year of lying in bed at university being a hungover mess, I decided that it had to stop. Following the steps laid out in the upcoming life hacks section, the negative effects of my hangovers were significantly decreased, and I managed to get things done the next day and feel relatively fresh. The methods I used to reduce the effects of the hangover were primarily trying to counteract all four major causes of a hangover previously mentioned: dehydration, vitamin and mineral depletion, acetaldehyde buildup and poor sleep quantity and quality. This model is not a miracle fix, but it will definitely help. If you drink alcohol, this could recover a significant number of days you would otherwise have spent in bed hating life.

Uni Lifehacks: From 'What You Should Take Before You Start Drinking' To 'Foods You Should Eat The Next Day To Help Your Body Recover'

What You Should Take Before You Start Drinking – Aspirin, it increases the amount of hangover reducing fatty acids (prostaglandins) that are in your system. And as a result, it has been shown to 'help with the hungover feeling of the next day' according to Dr Jeffrey Wiese, a Professor of Medicine at Tulane University and a hangover expert (34).

Clearer Drinks = Clearer Mornings – This is often cited as an old wives' tale, but there is now some science behind it. Clearer drinks, such as vodka and gin contain lower levels of congeners (impurities that are produced in the fermentation process) than darker drinks such as brandy, whisky, and tequila. Congener consumption is linked to the head or stomach ache you feel the day after drinking. A recent study by Alcoholism and Clinical Research tested 100 participants on the effects on congeners. In the study, two groups were given the same amount of alcohol, but one group was given a clear drink (vodka), and the other group were given a dark drink (whisky). The group who drank the darker drinks had far 'worse hangover effects than the group who drank clearer drinks'. In a similar study, 33% of those who drank bourbon reported a severe hangover in comparison to only 3% who drank the same amount of vodka! (35)

Stay Hydrated Throughout The Night – To avoid dehydration, have a glass of water every hour while you're on a night out. It's free from behind the bar and often tastes great when you are dehydrated from the dancing and the alcohol. (If the people you are with mock you for having a glass of water - remind yourself that you will have the last laugh tomorrow morning when they are in bed wanting to die.) An alternative way to stay hydrated is the infamous, 'Squadka'. Mix your alcohol (in this case vodka) with concentrated squash and water at pre-drinks, as this means that around 55-65% of the drink you're consuming is water. (You also get a reasonably tasty drink out of it too!)

Don't Drink Alcohol In The Final Hour – When you're out and the night is drawing to a close, it doesn't make much sense to buy another drink. All that will happen if you do is that you'll feel even more intoxicated on your way home, and push yourself over the edge into "seriously wasted" territory. That last drink could make the difference between waking up slightly worse for wear tomorrow, or waking up googling "can you die from a hangover?" Instead, in the final hour, try sticking to the water. Drink a couple of cups of water when you get in and leave a bottle of water next to the bed for when you wake up. If not, you'll regret it the next morning when you are crawling to the kitchen with a throat drier than Gandhi's sandals.

Take This Multivitamin Before Going To Bed – A product that I used during my time at university and had positive experiences with was 'DrinkWel – The Multivitamin for people who drink'.[11] It has loads of vitamins and minerals in it to help replenish what your body has lost after drinking alcohol:

A. *N-Acetyl-L-Cysteine* – Your liver detoxifies the alcohol by producing glutathione. N-A-C is known to speed up the body's production of glutathione.

B. *Vitamin B6* – A study found that supplementation of Vitamin B6 reduced hangover severity by approximately 50% in a group who had been drinking (36).

---

[11] DrinkWel doesn't work for everyone, nor is it a complete cure. The reason why we included it was because it offers a full re-fund on your first order if you feel no positive effects the next day.

C. *Milk Thistle* – This has been shown to have components that help protect liver cells from toxic chemicals and drugs (including alcohol!) (37).

Protect Your Sleep – With alcohol negatively affecting the quality of your sleep, it's much easier to be woken up by noise or light. Increase your chances of getting a good night sleep by popping in some earplugs, wearing an eye mask and shutting your blinds.

Foods You Should Eat The Next Day To Help Your Body Recover – Here are three foods to help your body's recovery process:

A. *Spinach* – Most people are deficient in magnesium, and binge drinking reportedly doubles its excretion rate! Your magnesium levels are reduced for days after drinking, and low levels are associated with feelings of anxiety and depression. Spinach (as well as other dark leafy vegetables) are an excellent source to help rebuild your depleted magnesium levels. Have lots of it the day after drinking alcohol (38).

B. *Eggs* – They have a high concentration of an amino acid (L-Cysteine) which helps your body breaks down the alcohol in your system. (Alternative sources that produce similar effects are oats, yoghurt or broccoli.)

C. *Bananas* – Due to the frequent urination that occurs when you drink, you lose a lot of potassium too, which is a mineral required for proper nerve and muscle function. Get a banana or two down you to top yourself up. (Alternative sources that boost your magnesium levels are orange juice, potatoes and avocados.)

Warning ⚠

The next Lifehack only works on light to moderate hangovers. Do not do this if you have a severe hangover – you will be sick!

Jump Up And Down For 2 Minutes – This may sound ridiculous, but bare with us. The last thing most people want to do when hungover is move, let alone jump up and down. Hear us out – this could be a game-changer. It all relates to the lymphatic system. It's not often talked about, but your lymphatic system plays a crucial role in your body. 'It bathes every cell, carries nutrients to the cells and takes waste products away; it is vital for your body's immune system and detoxification'. For your lymphatic system to be fully activated, your body has to be in movement. If you do not move your body, the 'cells are left stewing in their own waste products, starving for nutrients'. Research has found that jumping up and down (on a trampoline) increases lymph flow up to fifteen to thirty times and is much more effective than regular exercise at doing this (39). It's likely that you don't have a trampoline, but you can create similar effects by jumping up and down for two minutes. (Put on some positive music while you do it. Just make sure you lock your door as your flatmates may think you're having a moment if they catch a glimpse.)

Don't Hang Out With Other Hangover-ers – Emotions, just like our good friend 'Freshers' Flu', can be contagious. It's actually a well-documented psychological phenomenon called 'emotional contagion'. This is the theory that other people's emotions can literally rub off on us. You've probably experienced this before – you were in a great mood, and then you bumped into someone who was in a foul mood, leading you to be in a foul mood for the rest of the day too. Emotional contagion can have a massive impact when we are feeling hungover. If you hang around with people who are hungover and feeling sorry for themselves, guess what will happen? You'll feel more hungover and sorry for yourself. If all your flatmates are laid in bed moaning about their hangovers, make sure you put on some feel-good music, get out of that environment and go somewhere people aren't hungover. Stay away from negative hungover people when you're trying to get things done; much like you would stay away from someone who has the flu, it's contagious.

Cycle Your Caffeine Intake – If you minimise your caffeine intake to primarily consuming when you are hungover, you will feel its effects far more when you are in a desperate need of energy. This tip can take you from looking like you belong on the cast of *The Walking Dead* to a semi-functioning human being. (Important to note that caffeine is not a substitute for sleep but does help negate the effects of sleep deprivation in the short term if you have to get things done. Make sure you sleep plenty the night after to try and compensate for the absence of quantity and quality sleep from the previous evening.)

Take Detox Periods – If you drink alcohol regularly, you should try and schedule in some detox periods throughout university. Your liver is an amazing organ that naturally repairs itself with time; however, it must be given time without alcohol to repair. I found a very good time to have a detox period was when I was back home over the holidays.

Download 'Drunk Mode' – Looking at your messages and calls after a night of drinking can often be terrifying. Drunk Mode allows you to block individual contacts so you cannot ring or text them when you have had a few drinks. When you search a certain person in your phone, it changes their number to a false one as well as gives you reminders of why you shouldn't contact them. If you try and unblock the person on the app when the booze has kicked in, it requires you to do a complex maths equation which is hard to do whilst you are sober; never mind intoxicated.

PART FOUR

SOCIAL LIFE

The social aspect of university is arguably the most important part of the experience. If all you take away from your time at university is your degree, you've done yourself a disservice. University is a time to make amazing memories, new friends, try new things, and meet people who are different to yourself in ways you can't imagine. If I were only allowed to have either my degree or the experiences and memories of the people I met whilst at university, I would probably pick the latter because they changed me in a way that my studies did not.

Three chapters make up the *Social Life* part of this book. Chapter Ten is the most in depth as it is ultimately the foundation of your social life at university: *Become A Social Butterfly*. Without well developed social abilities, you'll struggle to have a fulfilling social life at university. This chapter looks at the two biggest lies society tells you about your social abilities, as well as two practices you can do to improve them.

The next chapter moves on to the topic of *The Night Out*. With most (not all) social occasions related to nights out, we take a look at how you can start your own event as a university student. There's also a collection of all the best night out Lifehacks, from throwing a memorable house party to paying just £1 for a taxi home!

The last chapter is called *Enjoy It*. As a student, you live in a period of time with immense freedom, where you can broaden your horizons and tick items off your bucket list. Make the most of this abundance of free time and lack of real responsibilities, before you have to face the constraints of the working world. When uni is finished, your free time will decrease, and your responsibilities will increase. This chapter explores ways you can maximise the great times you have at university, which you will look back and reflect on for years to come.

10

Become A Social Butterfly

"There are no strangers here;
only friends you haven't yet met."

–W.B. Yeats

"I regret all the times I spent having fun with my friends.
I wish I would've spent more time in my room alone."

–No Graduate Ever

Why Most Advice Given To Students About Their Social Life Is Useless

The main reason for writing this book, as mentioned in the introduction, was our frustration with the pointless advice that was given to us at university. There is no better example of this than the advice given to students regarding their social life. For example, most students (maybe even yourself) have been given the following advice by friends and family:

🖉 *"Just BE confident"*

- ✎ *"Be SOCIABLE"*
- ✎ *"Make as MANY friends as you can"*
- ✎ *"DON'T be nervous"*
- ✎ *"Introduce yourself to as MANY people as possible"*

This advice is all well and good, but like the majority of students, you probably already knew that this is 'what to do'. The issue isn't knowing what to do, but rather **how to do it**. There's isn't a student sat alone in the corner of a bar because they 'forgot to get rid of their nerves.' Nor is there a student who is struggling to meet people they really like because they 'forgot to look for them'. Telling someone to do these things when they don't have much experience doing it is about as valuable as telling a learner driver to *"just put the key in the ignition and drive"*. The advice may be well-intentioned, but it is ultimately useless to that person, and can sometimes actually set them back. With that in mind, in the remainder of this chapter, we've tried to steer clear of the clichéd advice, and instead look at genuinely useful action-oriented information (backed by personal experience and some scientific research) that we wish we'd been given.

The Two Biggest Lies Society Tells You About Your Social Abilities

1. **People Pay Attention To Everything You Do** – As we are at the centre of our own universe, it's very easy to fall into the trap of thinking that other people view us as the centre of their universe. However, logically this can't be true. They, just like us, are the centre of their own universe. They have their own ambitions, wants, worries and insecurities. The common misconception that people pay more attention to you than they actually do is

a well-documented psychological phenomenon known as the 'spotlight effect'. (Defined as 'the idea that people tend to believe they are being noticed more than they really are'.)

In a study of the spotlight effect, a group of university students were asked to wear an embarrassing t-shirt to one of their lectures. After their lectures had been over, the students who were wearing said embarrassing t-shirt were asked to estimate how many people in the lecture noticed their poor fashion choice. The researchers then asked the people in the lecture whether they noticed the t-shirt. It turned out that the students wearing the t-shirt estimated that twice as many people in the room noticed than was reported! (40) (41)

In social situations, it's so easy to get stuck in our heads worrying about how we are coming across to other people. This fear is natural and everyone experiences it to some extent, just look at what the number one human fear is. It's not heights, it's not spiders, and it's not even death… It's public speaking! Comedian Jerry Seinfeld has a very apt joke about it:

> *"According to most studies, people's number one fear*
> *is public speaking. Number two is death. Death is*
> *number two. Does that seem right? That means to*
> *the average person, if you have to go to a funeral,*
> *you're better off in the casket than doing the eulogy!"*

Public speaking, like most other social situations that we fear, can mean we spend a lot of time in our own heads, worrying about how we're being perceived. However, there's a truth that society doesn't tell you – people aren't all that interested in every little thing you do! Often they are too busy worrying about your opinions of them to even form an opinion of you. They didn't notice the coffee you spilt down yourself this morning because they were too busy worrying whether you've seen the enormous spot on their forehead.

The majority of people don't pay attention to everything you do, and the rest, probably don't pay any attention at all. We're all living our own lives, and have our own issues to deal with.

2. **You're Born With Your Social Abilities And You Can't Change Them** – Many people work under the premise that they either have good social abilities or they don't. Some people are just born with an innate ability to be charming, funny and the life of the party. Thankfully, this isn't the case. Well, it's not the case if you **believe** it's not the case.

   The way you view your traits and abilities can drastically affect whether they stay the same or improve. It sounds like a cheesy Instagram quote, but it's true. You can improve your social abilities, particularly your social skills and confidence if you believe you can. Carol Dweck, a Psychology professor at Stanford University, has been at the forefront of this research. She has found a remarkable growth in people's abilities when they make a mental change to the way they perceive things like their intelligence and personality. The two types of mindset identified by Dweck are a Fixed Mindset and a Growth Mindset:

   A. Fixed Mindset – People who view their abilities as innate and unalterable traits. i.e. *"I'm naturally a shy person, and I always will be shy."*

   B. Growth Mindset – People who view their abilities as malleable, able to be altered and improved with practice. i.e. *"I feel shy in social situations right now, however, with time and practice I can overcome this feeling."*

A recent study looked at the effects of adopting a growth mindset on the social lives of university students. In the study, Freshers were assessed before starting university on how they viewed their shyness. Seven months into their time at uni, the students who saw shyness as a fixed trait, that they couldn't change or overcome, showed an increase in their nerves in social situations. In contrast, the students who saw shyness as something malleable that could be overcome saw a decrease in their nerves in social situations! (42)

Imagine listening to someone say "*I can't ride a bike, it just doesn't come naturally to me.*" You'd probably laugh and say "*Riding a bike is something you need to practice to get good at and nobody is naturally good or bad at riding a bike*" The only thing holding them back from being able to ride a bike is their limiting belief that they cannot ride a bike.

Yet, how many times have you heard people say statements like, "*I'm just a naturally shy person*", "*I'm not great at making new friends*" or "*I can't handle rejection*"? These statements should seem just as ridiculous as somebody saying they can't ride a bike by nature. Imagine someone saying "*My hands weren't designed for handlebars*", "*I've not got the right legs for peddling*" or "*I can't handle falling off my bike.*" Cycling abilities, like social abilities, aren't fixed traits that you were given from birth like your eye colour. They are all skills that can be learnt and developed. If you struggle with social abilities, it's not necessarily because you're naturally bad, it's because you have never been taught about them or spent any time practising.[12]

If you are still sceptical about social abilities being something you can learn and develop, ask yourself, how many times in your life have you been taught about social abilities? How many classes

---

[12] That's not to say that social abilities aren't influenced by genetics and childhood experiences. Of course, they are. What we're is saying is that you can learn these traits and improve them regardless of your genetics and childhood experiences.

have you gone to? How many books have you read? If you are like most people, your answer will probably be zero.

When you realise that people aren't paying anywhere near as much attention as you think and that you can improve your social abilities, you feel truly liberated. I say all this from personal experience. I used to suffer from social anxiety before university and throughout my first year. I would live in my head and constantly be terrified about what people thought about me. There was always a voice at the back of my head analysing every word I said and every action I took. And I believed that's 'just who I am'. A situation like a first date or attending a large social gathering would scare the hell out of me, I would feel it deep in my stomach, my muscles would tense up, and my breathing would become shallow. It was a nightmare.

However, I decided that university had so many social opportunities; I couldn't afford to waste them. I spent hours reading about socialising and charisma and had an epiphany when I realised that people weren't paying attention to everything I did (or anything I did for that matter!) and that I wasn't born without any social abilities, they were things I could actively learn.

A 2 Minute Exercise Scientifically Proven To Make You Feel More Confident

Think back to a time where you felt confident and on top of the world. Maybe it was when you got your A-Level results, your sports team scored in the last minute, or you asked someone out, and they said yes. Go back to that moment and try and remember what your body language was like.

Now also think back to a time where you felt the complete opposite; it could have been when you got your A-Level results, your sports team conceded in the last minute, or you asked someone out, and they said no! Again, go back to that moment and try and remember what your body language was like.

How did your body language differ in the two instances?

When you feel confident, you tend to take up as much space as possible. The epitome of this is the victorious athlete celebrating with their chin up and hands in the air. When you aren't feeling confident, you do the reverse and take up as little space as possible. The epitome of this is the person with their chin tucked down, who stares at the floor with their shoulders hunched when talking to their crush in the library.

The real question is: Why do we do this? Did we learn it from the rest of society?

No.

Well not entirely. This behaviour may have been reinforced by other people, but these body language reactions are ingrained in **our very nature**. How do we know this? Because people who were blind from birth exhibit the exact same body language, despite obviously never having observed anybody else perform it. A study found that when congenitally blind athletes won a race, they reacted with their hands in the air, their chin went up, and they took up lots of space (43). According to Amy Cuddy, a Professor at Harvard Business School, body language is a form of 'nonverbal communication', and it exists throughout the animal kingdom. For example, the higher up a gorilla is in the social hierarchy, the more physical space it will try take up with its body to show its dominant position.

So, it's clear that how we feel affects our body language. But can the reverse be true? Could our body language affect how we feel? Professor Cuddy looked to test this hypothesis; could change in body language make someone feel more or less confident?

To test this she split participants into two groups, one group practised high confidence body language (hands in the air, chin up, shoulders back), and the other group practised low confidence body language (head down, shoulders slumped, eyes looking at the floor.) Both groups maintained their respective body language for just two minutes and were then given a series of tests to measure how confident they felt:

1. **Risk Taking** – From the participants who did the low confidence body language, only 16% of them were willing to take a risk. In stark contrast, out of the participants who did the high confidence body language, a whopping 86% of them were willing to take a risk.

2. **Changes In Hormones** – The participants were given swab tests before and after changing their body language to see whether there were any hormonal changes. (They looked at testosterone, the hormone associated with confidence, and cortisol, the hormone associated with stress and anxiety.)

   After just two minutes of displaying low confidence body language, the participants saw a 10% decrease in the confidence hormone (testosterone) and a 15% increase in the stress hormone (cortisol).

   Even more remarkably, the participants who did the high confidence postures and positions saw a 20% increase in the confidence hormone (testosterone) and a 25% decrease in the stress hormone (cortisol). That's a net difference of 30% and 40% in hormones associated with confidence, stress and anxiety, from just two minutes of body language changes!

3. **Job Interview Performance** – To further prove the effect that body language can have on the way we feel in high-pressure social interactions, Cuddy looked at one of the most nerve-wracking experiences – a job interview.

   Before two groups of participants went into a job interview, the researchers made them perform the high and low confidence body language poses. The group who did the high confidence body language pose beforehand were deemed to have performed 'substantially better' in the interviews than the group who did the low confidence one. (44)

How To Apply This At University – The Body Language Effect

1. **CHANGE your body language for two minutes before a big occasion –** Whether you have a big date or a presentation that you are worried about – simply do whatever confident body language you feel comfortable with behind closed doors for two minutes (or more!). For example, if you are in the shower beforehand, put your hands up in the air for two minutes, fully stretch out and keep your chin up.

2. **Be MINDFUL of negative body language –** Often in social situations when people get nervous or anxious, they will start to show it in their body language. The classic example is looking at your mobile phone in awkward social situations. The phone comes out, the chin drops and the shoulders hunch over. The body language someone has when they are on their phone is very similar to the low confidence body language mentioned in the research. That body language will make you feel more stressed out and less confident, which will lead to further negative body language and so on and so forth. It's a nasty cycle. If you catch yourself doing this, be mindful, stop it and change your body language. Take a deep breath and put your phone away (or at least bring it up, so your head is not down.)

How To Reduce Nerves By Regularly Getting Out Of Your Comfort Zone

Go back again to an experience where you felt really nervous and anxious in a social situation. It could be public speaking or getting ready for that first date. Instead of your body language, this time think about the physiological responses you felt. You probably experienced some of the usual suspects:

- Racing heart
- Sweaty palms
- Dry mouth
- Butterflies in your stomach
- Tensed muscles
- Shallow breathing
- Red cheeks
- Stuttering voice
- Light-headedness

Unlike body language, these are things that you cannot consciously control. These are unconscious reactions, and you cannot tell your heart to slow down or swat away those butterflies in your stomach. These physiological responses are caused by your Autonomous Nervous System (ANS). The ANS is controlled by your subconscious, and it produces these physiological reactions whenever it perceives that you are in danger. Take a racing heart for example. This is an incredibly useful biological too that's there for a reason. Your heart is pumping blood to your muscles and getting you ready to either fight or get the hell out of there. Our hunter-gatherer ancestors relied on this automatic reaction throughout their lives. The harmless log on the floor could actually be an enormous snake, and they'd need to move – sharpish! However, these evolutionary benefits don't always translate well into twenty-first-century life. There's no reason to be preparing to run or fight when you're talking to a stranger or answering a question in a packed lecture hall, but our body still reacts in the same way. The issue is that the autonomous nervous system *is* autonomous – by its very definition, you can't control it, it doesn't listen to logic or reason.

Instead, the most effective way to reduce your body's fear response in social situations is to put it in direct contact with the fear on a regular basis. When you overcome it, and nothing negative has happened to you, your ANS will gradually begin to reduce its fear response. The ANS begins to realise that the situation it is producing this physiological response to actually poses no real danger. This isn't just scientific mumbo jumbo. There are thousands of accounts online of the benefits of people doing exactly this; they call it Comfort Zone Challenges. This is where people actively put themselves in a situation they find uncomfortable to conquer their fear and desensitise their ANS's response (45). Getting out of your comfort zone can be very scary at first, but they'll create some of the greatest experiences and memories you will have while at university. Nobody looks back on uni and remembers the comfortable moments, lying in bed eating a jar of Nutella. It may feel damn good at the time, but it's the spontaneous nights out with friends, introducing yourself to a stranger who becomes a best friend, starting an event, acting in a play or running a marathon that people remember most fondly.

How To Apply This At University – Crushing Comfort Zones

1. **COMFORT ZONE challenges** – Look at which social situations cause you the most fear and design regular comfort zone challenges around them. Remind yourself with each comfort zone challenge completed, you will begin to become comfortable with what you previously found uncomfortable. If you keep this up throughout university, you will be unrecognisable to your former self by the end of it. Here are some ideas of some comfort zone challenges to try:

   - Lead a presentation in front of your seminar group

   - Refrain from untagging yourself from a photo on Facebook where you don't look your best

   - Ask five people out that you find attractive

   - Ask a question during your lecturer's Q&A

   - Go on a night out without drinking alcohol

   - Start a new hobby

   - Give blood

   - Sign up for a Jailbreak event or a long distance race

   - Go skydiving or bungee jumping

   - Join a new society and attend a social

   - Give a compliment to someone new each day

Uni Lifehacks: From 'How To Never Forget Anyone's Name' To 'How To Maximise Your Matches On Dating Apps'

How To Never Forget Anyone's Name – At university, you are going to meet a lot of new people, and it can be a real struggle to remember all their names. Here are some tips to avoid the awkward *"So sorry – what's your name again?"* or even worse, calling them the wrong name:

A. *Visual association* – Boris Nikolai Konrad is the world memory champion (yes that's a thing!) Konrad managed to memorise 280 words and 195 names and faces in fifteen minutes. He does it is by using visual imagery and associating the words, names and faces with pre-learned cues. Whenever you meet a new person, and you hear their name, try and create a visual link between their name and something it reminds you of. For example, if you were to meet someone called Tom, the first thing it may remind you of is Thomas the Tank Engine. You then picture this person as a gigantic talking train for a few seconds when you are interacting with them. Repeat it over and over in your mind until it sticks. Next time you see Tom, you'll automatically visualise the giant talking train, and you'll remember his name is Tom. It sounds ridiculous, but it works, and you will never forget his name.

B. *Repeat their name at the start of the conversation* – Alternatively, when they tell you their name, say it in the first few sentences of your conversation.

i.e. *"Nice to meet you, Lucy."*

"So Lucy, what are you studying?"

"Oh, so how do you know Ryan, Lucy?"[13]

---

[13] Don't use all of these however, pick one, or the person you're talking to will think you have lost the plot.

C. *The Facebook trick* – If you forgot to do the above and cannot remember their name after a long time talking to them, try the Facebook trick. *"Oh let me add you on Facebook."* Pass them your phone and let them search for themselves. They will then hand you your phone back with their profile and their full name.

Chew Your Nerves Away – If you are nervous before a social occasion, pop in some gum. Researchers conducted an experiment in which two groups were asked to perform the same stress-inducing tasks, except one group was chewing gum, and the other wasn't. The group chewing gum were found to have 18% less cortisol (the hormone associated with stress, anxiety and nerves) in their system! (46)

How To Maximise Your Matches On Dating Apps – A recent study reported that by 2031, 50% of relationships will be started through dating apps or online, and by 2041 it will rise to 70% of relationships. The number of 18-24-year-olds using these services has increased 170% in the last few years, and 69% of people are now comfortable going on a date with someone they met online or via their smartphone (47) (48) (49). So, it would be unfair not to mention Tinder, Bumble and all the other swiping apps out there. If you're in a relationship, skip this, or take some notes for your single swipe-a-holic friends:

A. *3+ pics and write a bio* – Use three or more pictures and write a bio. The research certainly backs it up. In an analysis of Tinder stats of almost 500,000 users, it was found that the profiles that had three or more pictures increased their chances of getting a match by 9-15% across both genders. In the same analysis, it was found that female profiles that had a bio garnered 58% more matches, and male profiles got an incredible 400% more matches as a result! (50)

B. *Fitted clothes > expensive clothes* – In a study done at the University of Hertfordshire, two groups were judged solely on their appearance. One group wore fitted clothes, and the other group wore poorly-fitted expensive clothes. The group with the fitted yet cheaper clothes was judged to be more attractive than the group wearing the more expensive non-fitted clothes, despite the fact the faces of both groups were blurred out (51).

C. *Wear red* – Irrespective of culture, people love the colour red. A study published in the Journal of Experimental Psychology found that female participants continually ranked the men wearing red as more attractive than their counterparts wearing other colours. The study was repeated in England, Germany, USA and China with the same results each time. Similarly, another study found that women wearing red were 'far more likely to get messages and dates than those wearing any other colour'. (It's also been found that men who wear red appear to be more successful and confident, and waitresses wearing red receive more tips.) (52)

D. *Don't smile* – This goes against a lot of advice that is given out, but a smirk or a gaze achieves greater results than a smile. An analysis of over 7,000 photos found that the men and women who didn't smile in their pictures got a greater response rate than those who did. (53)

E. *Get the pup* – Having a dog when asking for a phone number increased the chances of getting said phone number by 300% in one study! In another study, 35% of women and 26% of men stated that they had been more attracted to someone because they owned a pet, with dog owners deemed the most attractive of the lot. (It's also an easy way for the other person to open up a conversation with you.) (54)

F. *Don't cross your arms* – Researchers created two profiles for the same individuals. One profile showed the photos of the person having open body language, (chin up, arms in the air, reaching out to grab something) and the other showed them with closed body language (crossed arms or hunched shoulders). The profile with the open body language gained considerably more interest than the closed body language profile, despite being the same person (55).

G. *Get the guitar* – A study published in *Letters On Evolutionary Behavioral Science* looked at the effects that a guitar can have on someone's attractiveness. The same person approached 300 people for their phone number. For each approach, they either had a gym bag, a guitar or nothing in their hands. When the participants had the guitar, they were three times more likely to get the phone number compared to when they had a gym bag, and twice as likely to get the number compared to when they had nothing in their hand (56). (Obviously, this is going to backfire if you're lying and they ask you to play them a rendition of Paolo Nutini later down the line. Instead, include in your profile a photo that showcases your creative side – something which you actually can do!)

H. *Link it to your Instagram* – This will help prove you are a real person and alleviate their worries about ending up on an episode of MTV's *Catfish*.

I. *The two f's* – Always try and follow the golden rule of 'Funny or Food'. GIFs or humorous openers have found to increase the chances of the other person responding by 30%, and a mention of food gained a 40% increase.

J. *Optimise your time* – Tinder (and all the other swiping apps) are reportedly at their busiest between 5 PM and midnight, with

Sunday being the busiest day of the week. To gain the greatest traction and return on investment, get messaging and swiping during these periods.

Join As Many Sports Clubs And Societies As You Can – From writing this book and interviewing students, this is the number one recommendation that comes up again and again. Even if you only attend a few introductory sessions and decide to be purely a social member, this will widen your social circle every single time you do it. This is possibly the easiest way to meet people who aren't on your course or who don't live in your accommodation.

How To Persuade People – You may want to get your untidy and reluctant flatmate to clean the living room. Or, maybe your mate is about to flake on the event you were planning on going to. In these situations, our natural tendencies are to try and persuade them to do what we want by telling them how disgusting the living room is or how great the event is going to be. Instead of giving your reasons as to why they should do something, you should instead try and tap into their own motivations by asking these two irrational questions. Let's use the night out example:

> *"On a scale of 1-10, how much do*
> *you want to go to that event tonight?"*

As they are reluctant, they will probably give you a number between two and four. Let's say they reply with the number three. They will be expecting you to respond with, *"What? A three?! Why aren't you a ten! It's going to be such a good night!"*. Instead of responding like that, try and answer with the counterintuitive question of:

> *"Why didn't you pick a lower number?*
> *Why aren't you a 2?"*

They will then begin to respond with their own reasons for not going to the event. They may respond with *"I'm not a 2 because I've not got anything due this week"*. Or, *"I'm not a 2 because the line-up is actually really good"*.

This is the key to persuasion according to Daniel Pink, persuasion expert and best-selling author on the subject. Get the person you're trying to convince to acknowledge their own reasons for doing something. They will believe their own reasons far more than any argument you could give to them, no matter how convincing. Once you've got that initial momentum of them convincing themselves of the idea, it's much easier to start persuading them to do it.

Hold on, you may be thinking, what if they are super reluctant. What if they responded with *"I'm a one, there's no way I'm going tonight "*? Try this response: *"What's stopping you from being a two? What can I do to make you a two?"*. They then may respond with *"Well I'm absolutely penniless, so there's no way I can afford it."* or *"There's no way I could get ready in time, I've got to make dinner, have a shower, do my makeup and decide on what to wear."* According to Pink, when somebody is a 1/10, there is usually an 'environmental obstacle in front of them'. In the case above, the environmental obstacle was their lack of money to buy a ticket or time to organise themselves. When you know what's stopping them, you can resolve the issues they face (i.e. pay for their ticket or cook them dinner) and persuade them towards your cause, whether that be cleaning the kitchen, or going on a night out. Pink says *"The key is that we tend to think of persuasion as something that one person does to another"* whereas it's actually about bringing out *"people's own reason for doing something."* (57)

11

The Night Out

"Well, I'm having a good time. Which makes
me feel guilty too… How very English."

–David Attenborough

"No one looks back on their life and
remembers the night they had plenty of sleep."

–Unknown

How To Start Your Own Event On A Student Budget

Starting an event certainly offers loads of social benefits and helps to establish your name on campus. It is often assumed that you need capital to start this kind of venture and while money helps, it isn't a prerequisite. In this chapter we'll show you how to start your own event, without stacks of cash:

1. **Have a USP** – Think outside the box and make sure the event you are planning has a unique selling point to differentiate it from the current options in your city. It could be as simple as

a curating and playing a genre of music that no other venue or event in your university town or city is playing. A good source of ideas is to look at other cities and see what is working there that doesn't yet exist where you are. Be careful though, the same idea may not work as well in Bangor as it will in Birmingham! If the city you observe is of a similar size with similar demographics, the likelihood is that there will also be demand in your own city and a gap for you to exploit.

2. **Perform Market Research** – Ask lots of students and get feedback on your idea. Do they like it? What would be the best venue for it? What would be the best date for it? How can you make this event extra special for them? If the research says it won't work, find out why and adapt your plan accordingly. Always listen to the marketplace. i.e. If it's the best idea for a night ever, but you plan to start it midway through the exam period, it's maybe not the best idea.

3. **Contact Venues and Events Companies** – Show them the research and the passion that you have for the project. Try and negotiate a deal that will offer them considerable value such as a percentage share of ticket sales and sales of drinks behind the bar to make it worth their while. This strategy may be more difficult in larger cities with a more established nightlife or events scene so you may have to do a fair bit of networking.

4. **Find An External Sponsor** – If venues are not taking you seriously, or are asking for too much money, contact local companies about your plan and offer them advertising at your event in return for money and/or free products or services. Think outside of the box. You could team up with an app whose target market are university students, and if people show the app at the door of your event, they get in for free or receive a free drink.

In return, the app gives you a certain amount of money for the advertisement you are providing to make it worth your while. Ensure that the company's customer demographic fits with the type of people that are attending your night to enhance your chances of success. If you are looking to put on an underground grime night, it doesn't make sense to look for sponsorship from the local retirement home.

5. **Hire Local Acts** – Don't look to hire big name artists initially, as you will need a lot of cash up front. Hire local ones, as they will be much cheaper and are looking for a platform to get their name out there. Make it part of the agreement that they will bring a certain amount of friends to your event if they are to perform there to help boost ticket sales.

6. **Target Societies and Sports Clubs** – Draw up a list of ten of the biggest sports teams and societies at your university and get in contact with their committee about bringing everyone down to your event. Getting the committee on-side is crucial as they bring the rest of the members with them. You could offer them perks such as free entry and an incentivised reward (e.g. a free gift from your sponsor or a bottle of vodka) if they bring a certain amount of their members to the event.

Uni Lifehacks: From 'Throwing A Memorable House Party' To 'How To Pay Just A Pound For A Taxi Home'

Predrinks Hacks:

A. *Cool your drinks in half the time* – If you have a drink that is lukewarm that you would like to drink sharpish, wrap a wet paper towel around it and stick it in the fridge. Your drink will be chilled after 15-20 minutes.

B. *Make your own drinks cooler* – Fill your washing machine with ice, this can act as a cooler that you can leave your drinks in.

C. *Get some portable Bluetooth speakers* – There's nothing that kills a vibe quite like someone playing music out of their phone like 'that guy' on the back of a public bus! Invest in some Bluetooth speakers. They are relatively inexpensive, will last you the entirety of university and you can move them wherever you want.

Throwing A Memorable House Party:

A. *Individual messages > group messages* – People tend to ignore group messages, which will make your house party seem dead as 'fifty people have read this', but nobody has responded. Instead, send out an individual message to each person. It can even be copied and pasted, but people are way more likely to message you back and actually turn up when you have made that personal connection with them.

B. *Weather* – Rain has been known to reduce the number of people that will even attend a funeral. Moral of the story – try and avoid a rainy day if you can.

C. *Date* – Don't pick dates near exams or deadlines. Don't pick the same date as a big event or the day after, as people will choose that event or still be hungover from it, no matter how close you are to them.

D. *Be creative* – Pick a hilarious or unique theme. Think outside the box and do something that will get people talking.

E. *Stagger the invites* – With the first thirty invites, ask people who you know are definitely going to click attending. Then start inviting the other people; when people see that the event is already popular, they are more likely to click going and actually attend.

F. *Cost* – Reduce costs by working with a company. Look at businesses that are marketing towards students and see whether you can work together. Certain apps have been known to pay the party thrower if people show the app at the door to your house party. You can even get in touch with student ambassadors of big brands like Red Bull or Smirnoff (if your area has them) who may provide free drinks at your party.

G. *Avoiding an ASBO* – Knock on your neighbours' doors on the day of the house party and let them know that you will be doing some 'birthday celebrations'. Be super friendly and give them your number. They will be way far less likely to call the council or police later that night when they've had a positive experience with you. (My house was one step away from an ASBO within the first week of living there, and after doing this, we never had a noise complaint ever again.)

Get Their Facebook Instead Of Their Number – If you meet somebody you like on a night out, get them on Facebook instead of asking for their number. Why?

A. *Your photos will trigger their memory of you* – They will be able to put a face to a name the next morning, rather than wondering who the '+44…' number that texted them was.

B. *Conversation starting points* – Maybe they are mutual friends with somebody you know from home, or they work at the bar you usually go to.

C. *It's more consensual* – If the person wasn't into you and was just being polite, they don't have to accept your friend request. Whereas with a number, they are giving you the ability to get a hold of them whenever!

D. *Beer goggles do exist* – You can both view Facebook photos sober the next day.

Credit Card Roulette – If you've been brave enough to avoid our advice about leaving the debit card at home, then this is possibly one of the funniest (and financially damaging) games you can play on a night out.

Everyone orders a drink at the bar, let's say there are six people and they each get a beverage of their choice. When the bartender asks for payment, they offer everyone's debit cards, and the bartender is told to pick one at random. Whichever card they choose has to pay for the whole round. If you win, you get a free drink, however, if you lose, you lose big. (I had a friend who gave his bus pass instead of his debit card. Double check they are all bank cards before playing, and someone isn't sneaky!)

No B.S. Dating Advice That Actually Works On A Night Out:

A. *Confidence is key* – It's a cliché, but it's true; confidence, again and again, is deemed an attractive personality trait irrespective of gender or culture. A study of all the research on attraction showed that men and women universally deem confidence to be 'very attractive' in a potential partner. In one very unethical study, a group of male actors were told to treat an unknowing, shy and unconfident female university student as though they found her 'extremely attractive' whenever they saw her around campus. She was not aware that the male students were actors, and with the interest she received, her confidence around campus grew as a result. The results were astonishing. Before the study, the girl received very little romantic interest. However, as her confidence grew, so did her dating options. All of a sudden, other male university students, (who weren't actors or even aware of the study!) suddenly found the girl with new-found confidence much more attractive. These guys went from barely noticing the girl to regularly asking her out. Dr Craig Malkin, a Harvard psychologist and expert on confidence, noted that 'the more self-assured she was, the more open and confident she was with men, the more attractive she became'.

In another bizarre study, male participants were split into two groups – with one subtle difference; one group was given deodorant, and the other group wasn't. A group of women were asked to rate the attractiveness of the two groups in still photos and video footage. When they saw the still photos, there was no difference in attractiveness reported by the women between the deodorant and non-deodorant group. However, after watching video footage, the women reported finding the deodorant group significantly more attractive – despite the fact they couldn't even smell them! How could this be? During the study, the two male groups were asked to report their levels of confidence. As you'd expect, the deodorant group reported higher levels of confidence than the non-deodorant group. The difference between the still photos and the video footage was that the later enabled the women to see those signs of confidence that they couldn't see in the still photos (e.g. body language and eye contact.) (58) (59)

B. *Be a social butterfly when you are out* – Firstly, don't make your night dependent on meeting Miss or Mr Right, instead make it about being a social butterfly and having fun. Meeting that one person isn't in your control, but having a good time always is. Make it your aim to be the person having the best time in the room. When people notice that you are having a good time, it will rub off on them, and they will want to spend more time around you. Chat to as many people you can, and this starts even before the night out. Chat with everyone at pre-drinks, the taxi driver, the people in the queue for the club or bar, the door staff, the person you are paying entry to and the person behind the bar when you buy your first drink. Be friendly and have a joke with them. Compliment people. Build up other people's confidence and self-esteem.

Why does this work? Doing this in the lead up to the night out will get you more relaxed and put you in a sociable mood, and this will be reflected in the vibe you give off for the rest of the evening. Everyone is always naturally drawn to the person having the most fun in the room.

C. *Start a conversation with ten people you find attractive when you are out* – Make this a fun goal to complete throughout the night. Notice this is not saying you have to try and get their number or arrange a date, it is merely starting a conversation by **saying hello**. The aim is purely saying 'hey', and anything after that is a bonus. Why does this work? You'll be more confident because the more you chat with people, the more your fear will go away. When you say hello, you've already won. You have accomplished your goal of facing your fears and just saying hello. You don't need anything else to validate yourself. You have no expectations. You don't need to get their number or for them to fall in love with you. You are completely outcome independent. If it doesn't go perfectly, it's only 10% of your interactions for that night. This will produce a level of confidence that will be apparent during your interactions. It is a positive perpetual cycle that will result in you feeling more and more confident as the night goes on. The good news is that even though it wasn't your aim to meet someone you find attractive whose feelings are reciprocal – you are likely to due to your confidence and the good old law of averages! If you chat to ten people you find attractive, something similar to this might occur:

- ℘ Three of them are in a relationship or seeing someone.

- ℘ One of them has just got out of a long-term relationship and is not interested in dating right now.

- ℘ Two of them don't see you as dating material.

- ℘ Two of them weren't actually your type.

That leaves you with two people who you find attractive who are equally interested in you, which is one more than you need!

Stay Safe On Your Nights Out – Download Bsafe. It's an app that allows friends and family to view your journey home via GPS tracking. If you press the app's alarm in an emergency situation, they will be alerted, and the phone will start video and audio recording the situation in case the police ever need it as evidence.

How To Pay Just £1 For A Taxi Home – If you don't have enough money to get a taxi and a take-a-way, try combining both. This is a trick some friends and I did a few times at university.

Find a takeaway near to where you are that delivers, call them up and ask for delivery to your house. After you have made the order on the phone, ask if they can give your friend a lift from the takeaway shop as they have all your money. You then get in the takeaway car when it's about to deliver the goods to your house. Most delivery companies only charge £1 for delivery so it will be the cheapest taxi you will ever get.[14]

---

[14] This isn't guaranteed to work all the time, nor is it the safest, but it is hilarious. Just remember that your safety is more important than a cheap cab fare!

Enjoy It!

"Dost thou love life? Then do not squander time,
for that's the stuff life is made of."

–Benjamin Franklin

"Do not take life too seriously.
You will never get out of it alive."

–Elbert Hubbard

How to Fill Your Free Time With Experiences You Won't Forget

At university, you have the freedom to do anything you want. Don't let it go to waste. Ultimately your fondest moments aren't likely to be the hours spent working in the library or sweating yourself to death in the gym. Yes, getting your degree and staying healthy is important, but don't let it be all that you do. Instead, make the most out of the short period of time that you have and create as many memorable experiences as possible. What you define as a memorable experience will be up to you, but here are some ideas:

1. **Experience Live Entertainment** – Take every opportunity possible to experience as much live entertainment as you can. Whether this is in your city or halfway across the country, live entertainment is always memorable. Find out when your favourite musicians are touring, get your tickets in advance and if you have to, travel to see them. (Travel can be organised relatively cheaply, Megabus and the 16-25 Railcard will allow you to get around the country for a marginal sum.) Similarly, if there any stand-up comedians, live TV shows, events, theatrical productions or sports teams you have always wanted to see, university is the perfect time to go. Try and see some live entertainment that you haven't before; when you go into something with no idea what to expect it can produce some of the most memorable and enjoyable experiences. (*If you are strapped for cash, there are likely to be lots of local events on that will be reasonably cheap too.)

2. **New Activities With Friends** – This will produce some of the funniest and fondest memories of your time at university. These activities are also great bonding experiences that help bring your relationships closer. Potential ideas are endless, from bowling to camping (or 'Glamping' if you need your home comforts), from paintballing to a pottery class. Even if it's a letdown or the weather is awful, it will still give you plenty of hilarious stories.

3. **Challenge Yourself** – Not all great memories had at uni are the result of immediate pleasures like the ones listed above. A lot of memorable occasions can come from times of discipline where you pushed beyond what you thought your limits were. Try to conquer your fears and do something you always wanted to do or never even thought of doing. Act in a play, write a novel or get in the best shape of your life. Whatever it is, you will grow as a person as a result.

4. **Try As Many New Things As You Can** – If there is anything you have ever wanted to try before, university is the perfect time to give it a go. The worst that can happen is that you realise it was not for you. New experiences could come in the form of attending a 'Hot Yoga' or Brazilian Jiu Jitsu class. It could be as simple as trying food. You may find something you are passionate about that you would've never discovered otherwise.

5. **Travel** – A lot of students go travelling in the summer, visiting different places across the world. Think of places that you would like to go with friends and start planning. If you aren't lucky enough to have the cash to travel abroad, try a cheaper alternative and stay in the UK. Visit your uni friend's hometown or your home friend's uni town. It's not quite a Full Moon party in Koh Samui or interrailing across Europe, but a day and night out in Liverpool aren't half bad.

6. **Do Something Nice** – Some of the fondest memories come from when you're not thinking about yourself, but instead thinking about other people. Doing something nice could come in the form of throwing a friend a surprise birthday party, donating blood or buying a meal deal for the homeless guy you always see. It sounds clichéd, but if you make someone else feel good, you'll feel better too.

How To Apply This At University – Making Uni More Memorable ☺

1. **Draw up a BUCKET LIST** – Look at the six categories from the list above. Think of one thing you can do this year in each category.

2. **Draw up the next THREE STEPS you can take to make it happen** – i.e. 'Go Travelling – I want to go interrailing across Europe this summer. Here are three next steps to take:

   🎓 Chat with a friend who went on a similar trip and get an idea of how much it will cost.

   🎓 Create a Whatsapp group with friends from university or home and invite them.

   🎓 Set a date to have it all booked and paid for.'

3. **Take ACTION** – Do something tangible that will prevent you from being able not to do it. If you want to attend an event, book the tickets now. If you want to run a marathon, sign up straight away! (It also helps if you tell people what you are going to do so they can hold you accountable.)

4. **Create REMINDERS** – Put them everywhere, on your phone, near where you work or on your dresser. Put them in a place where they will regularly be seen, so you will constantly be reminded

Uni Lifehacks: From 'Netflix On Steroids' To 'The Secret That Cinemas Don't Want You To Know'

Netflix On Steroids:

A. *Netflix Enhancement Suite* (Chrome) – This little gem will give you ratings from IMDb and Rotten Tomatoes when you are on Netflix. These two sites are regarded as the most reliable for reviews and will ensure you don't waste your precious Netflix time watching something subpar. The plugin also gives you the ability to watch trailers for the shows you are considering watching.

B. *Flix Assist* (Chrome) – This will take your Netflix efficiency to whole new level. It automatically skips the opening and closing credits as well as the fifteen-second countdown for the next episode.

C. *Flix Roulette* (*www.netflixroulette.net*) – Do you spend more time searching for shows on Netflix than actually watching them? Flix Roulette will choose something at random for you. (You can choose a minimum star rating and preferred genre to stop yourself from sitting through something dire.)

D. *Rabbit* (*www.rabb.it*) – Maybe your best friend is at a uni on the other side of the country, your boy-or-girlfriend lives at home, or you can't be bothered with the five-minute walk to your mate's house. Rabbit is like Skype for Netflix, it links up your viewing so you are watching the show at the same time and has a chat function so you can message one another while you watch it.

Make Your AUX Cable Wireless – Get an Amazon Fire Stick or a Google Chromecast and stream your laptop or phone onto your TV screen.

Use Groupon For Money Off Activities – This one's a little obvious, but I found it so useful at uni. It gives you pages upon pages of great activities and experiences to do, whether it's paintballing, skydiving or immersing yourself in a sensory deprivation tank. Not only that, all of the activities are heavily discounted, meaning a lot of them are affordable on a student budget.

The Secret That Cinemas Don't Want You To Know –You are allowed to bring your own food and drink into their movies. It doesn't violate any of their rules, and it will probably save you a fortune. (This doesn't apply to hot food and alcohol).

THE ULTIMATE STUDENT SMOOTHIE[15]

This is to cheat meals what Mozart is to classical music:

INGREDIENTS
3 scoops of Häagen-Dazs Ice Cream
Two sticks of Kinder Bueno
100ml of milk
Handful of strawberries

METHOD
1. Break up the chocolate bar, and add the ice cream and the chocolate bar chunks to the blender.
2. Add the milk; if it is too thick, add a little more.
3. Add the strawberries
4. Blend until smooth

---

[15] This comes from Dave's uni flatmate Charlie Winterburn.

PART FIVE

INSIGHTS

Insights From Some Of The UK's
Most Successful Students

There's a reason why this book isn't called 'How To Uni'. Trying to advise everyone on 'how to do university properly' is impossible; each individual will have different interests, ambitions and desires, so there is no one-size-fits-all approach. With that in mind, we decided to interview some of the UK's most successful students, to find out their habits, tips and the lessons they learnt whilst at university. Whatever the path you are looking to take, we've tried to find people who excelled in many different industries and fields. These insights come from student musicians who have created globally played music, student-athletes who won accolades on the national and international stage, student journalists who have interviewed major figures including Prime Ministers and world famous actors, the student writers behind published books and popular blogs, student entrepreneurs who have set up exciting start-ups and students now employed by major firms. It also includes a whole host of students who balanced their degrees alongside raising thousands of pounds for charity, building up social media empires or battling and overcoming physical or mental illnesses.

One of the most interesting parts of interviewing these incredible students was finding out how they had achieved what they had. We aimed to give as much tangible advice as we could through these interviews. So, if you want to DJ in front of a sold-out crowd, start a charity that drastically improves people's lives, or just get a degree before tackling the real world, there are tips and tricks in all of these for you.

We categorised the insights into sections to make the book flow better. This is no way an attempt to pigeon hole anyone, most of these people can fit into more than one of the categories, with some even being able to fit into every single one of them. They offered a whole host of perspectives, from people pursuing a range of different goals, from diverse backgrounds, who all had different stories to tell. We hope you will find as much value in reading what these students have to say, as we did in hearing it.

Creatives

"If you find yourself asking yourself (and your friends), 'Am I really a writer? Am I really an artist?' Chances are you are. The counterfeit innovator is widely self-confident. The real one is scared to death."

–Steven Pressfield

"Ideas are like rabbits. You get a couple and then learn how to handle them, and pretty soon you have a dozen."

–John Steinbeck

DJing At Tomorrowland, Releasing My First Remix Globally on Sony Music and Ministry of Sound, and Having My Record Label's Work Recognised By David Cameron (All Alongside My Medicine Degree!)

—KISHAN BODALIA

NAME: Kishan Bodalia
UNIVERSITY: University of Birmingham
DEGREE: Medicine (MBChB)

Kishan Bodalia *(FB: @Bodaliamusic, www.bodalia.co.uk)* is a twenty-one-year-old medical student and DJ who has received acclaim in the international dance music scene. Kishan was named the winner of the Mazda Drives: The Sound of Tomorrow DJ competition for his 'unique, high energy and captivating' sound. He was subsequently selected by Mazda, the Lost Frequencies and Tomorrowland representatives to perform at Tomorrowland 2016. In the same year, he saw his first official remix *Daylight* released globally on Sony Music and Ministry of Sound, as well as being supported by BBC Introducing. Kishan is also the director of the expanding UK Record Label New Street Records – The world's first student-led record label and received the Points of Light award from then British Prime Minister David Cameron for his work helping and supporting aspiring student artists to reach their full potential.

Starting Out As A Student DJ

"Getting events as an unknown DJ, having never played a gig before was a considerable challenge for me. I didn't know who to contact, what to say and most importantly, I didn't know what they wanted to hear. In January 2015, I became involved in a new start-up company, New Street Records: the UK's first student-led record label, aiming to sign, record and promote the best student talent. In my role as

Head of Marketing at the time, I secured interviews on BBC radio and television, discussing the label and its objectives. I had the idea to team up with an existing event in another city as an opportunity to showcase our label outside of Birmingham. An interested friend of a friend provided me with the contact details of a Manchester-based club promoter. Days later, I secured my first slot at one of the world's most prestigious clubs – Sankey's, Manchester."

The Importance Of Social Media and Networking

"Social media plays a crucial role in accessing the largest number of people as quickly as possible – this is where I focused my attention. After much reading and experimenting, I have realised that understanding each social media platform can dramatically improve engagement. For example, on Facebook, being aware of the algorithms that underpin each type of post (such as text only, a photo, video or link to another website) and how this affects the reach is useful to recognise. There are many interesting online articles, supported by statistics, discussing this for many social media platforms. Expressing your professionalism through marketing techniques and conveying your personality means that people will engage with your brand on a more personal level. This could simply be in the form of responding warmly to comments and feedback, meaning that people will be more likely to interact with your content in the future. Striking this balance is also important in networking. It is natural that if a person is approachable and interesting, others will be more attracted and interested in what you do. This is likely to give you the edge in building relationships."

Take A Break!

"When working on creative projects, it's very easy to spend days in front of a computer screen without a break – as you make more progress, you work harder and longer to get closer to finishing the track. The times when I have motivated myself to take a day off or exercise, I'm far more productive when I get back in the studio. Also, when I take a break from a track for a few weeks, this allows the ideas to settle, and I can revisit it with a clear head to make any final tweaks. I tend to be most productive when I am most awake during the daytime, but often I'll stay up ridiculously late if I'm particularly excited about a track!"

Time Management Techniques Of A DJ Studying Medicine

"Time management is one of the biggest challenges at university as there is so much on offer. Studying medicine is time-consuming, and I attempt to balance my musical commitments around my academic work. My strategy to tackling endless amounts of work is to structure my time. I have an ongoing to-do list, which I continually add to with corresponding deadlines for each task. I then plan my work a day or two ahead, allocating certain jobs for each evening. Admittedly, I often make changes on the day, but having a framework to work within helps me to manage time. During busy periods like exams, I can easily go several weeks without making music. I do still have ideas coming into my mind during these busy weeks; I'm just unable to sit down for a period of time and apply them to my music. For this reason, I keep a list of ideas written as notes on my phone so that, when I have free time, I am able to quickly start making music with a goal in mind."

What's the funniest moment from your time at university?

"During the final of the DJ competition in Barcelona, all contestants had to perform on a yacht. A small stage had been created out of some flight cases to stand on. I played during a very turbulent spell, resulting in a couple of falls off the side of the stage – it added to the entertainment!"

Publishing Two Novels With HarperCollins And Having My First Book Labelled 'The Catcher In The Rye Of The Digital Age' By The Times

–ALICE OSEMAN

NAME: Alice Oseman
UNIVERSITY: Durham University
DEGREE: English Literature (BA)

Alice Oseman *(TW/IG: @aliceoseman, www.aliceoseman.co.uk)* is an author of young adult fiction. Publishing giant HarperCollins published Alice's first novel *Solitaire* when she was just nineteen years of age and her second novel *Radio Silence* was published in 2016. Alice's two books have revolved around the two teenage characters 'Tori Spring' and 'Frances' in *Solitaire* and *Radio Silence* respectively. Alice's work has received critical appraise leading her to be featured in The Guardian, BBC Breakfast, and the Times labelling one of her novels 'The Catcher in the Rye of the digital age'.

How Alice Became An Author

"Being an author seemed like such a mysterious, impossible thing that I didn't even consider the idea that I could do it. But after starting to write the novel that would eventually become my debut, *Solitaire*, I realised how desperately I wanted other people to read this story, and how being an author was the only career in which I could imagine myself truly happy. And so, from around sixteen years old, as I was writing *Solitaire*, I spent months researching online how one could become an author. I was completely obsessed with the idea. It consumed my thoughts every single day. After that, the process seemed rather simple, despite relying so heavily on luck. I had to send a part of my manuscript, along with a synopsis and a query letter, to literary agents, and hope that they liked my book enough to represent me and want to help me find a book publisher."

Write The Book You Want To Read

"Learning to write well can be a long process of trial-and-error. In the book I wrote before Solitaire, I didn't even know how to properly use dialogue punctuation. It's hard to really identify what qualifies as a 'mistake', because the 'mistakes' – the dodgy dialogue, description, structuring, pacing, characterisation, etc. taught me a new lesson, and contributed to my improvement as a writer. And I'm still learning! Every story I write is a little better than the last. The best piece of advice I have ever received is to write the book that you want to read. Your first reader is always going to be yourself, and if you enjoy what you're writing, then chances are there will be other people out there who enjoy it too. And if you're writing something that you love and are passionate about, that will undoubtedly translate into a more exciting, more vibrant novel."

Getting Published At A Young Age

"To be published with a traditional publisher, you first need to acquire a literary agent to represent you, as traditional publishers – A.K.A. the publishers that can get your books into nationwide bookshops – do not accept submissions from writers themselves. Getting the attention of literary agents, first of all, relies so heavily on luck. I just happened to send out a manuscript to an agent who was looking for a manuscript just like mine at the time. However, having a high-quality agency submission is of course very important. There is so much information online about agency submissions, and often different agents want different things (so check their websites!), but usually it involves sending a query letter, the first three chapters or ten-thousand words of your manuscript, and a concise synopsis of the novel. Each of these should be formatted in very specific ways, so again, internet research is absolutely vital! I advise sending out as many as you can (although always tell the agents in the query letters that you are undergoing 'simultaneous submissions' if you do so)."

How Alice Deals With Writer's Block

"The way I deal with writer's block is to simply stop writing for a while and go and get inspired by other things. For me, that could mean watching a few interesting films, listening to an album, playing a video game or going to the theatre. Usually consuming a few other cool things that people have made really makes me want to get back to making my own thing, and it encourages me to take different creative approaches or make different creative decisions. Writer's block can be particularly difficult when you're a student, as you already have so many pressures on you that can decrease your motivation to write. I can only recommend what I already have above, and also say that writing does not need to be inferior to your studies, or social life, even if you feel it might have to be. If writing is important to you, give it the time it deserves. When it comes to staying productive – I started writing a daily to-do list on a white-board I'd hung up in my room every evening for the next day. It kept me from having to wake up the next morning and think, *"Oh God, what do I need to do today!?"* Being a university student relies so heavily on time management that you can only get so far with a carefree attitude, trust me, I tried! And the satisfaction of crossing things off a to-do list truly never gets old."

Co-Founding An Award Winning Economics Magazine
–MUSTAFA REHMAN

NAME: Mustafa Rehman
UNIVERSITY: King's College London
DEGREE: Political Economy (BSc)

Mustafa Rehman graduated with a first-class degree in Political Economy from King's College London. He was nominated by the Department of Political Economy to receive the 2016 Jelf Medal – King's College London's highest student honour – for his academic achievements and services to the university. In his first year, he won an Undergraduate Research Fellowship at the Institute of Psychiatry, Psychology, and Neuroscience where he participated in research taking place in the areas of Experimental Economics and Neuroeconomics. He co-founded and was the Editor-in-Chief of *Perspectives*, an award-winning economics magazine that promotes interdisciplinary investigation into topical issues such as inequality and growth. Contributors to the publication include senior figures at The World Bank, the IMF, and Harvard University. He also served as the President of the KCL Economics & Finance Society and was responsible for hosting and interviewing a number of prominent speakers such as Yanis Varoufakis, (former Finance Minister of Greece) David Halpern, (Director of the UK Government's "Nudge Unit") and Diane Coyle (former Vice Chairman of the BBC). In his final year at university, Mustafa completed internships in four corporate law firms: Slaughter and May, Cleary Gottlieb Steen & Hamilton, Jones Day, and White & Case. He is now working at the global law firm Linklaters.

The 3 Questions To Ask Yourself Before Starting A Creative Project

"Firstly, do you have a team of people that you can trust? The single most important asset in any organisation is the amount of trust present between its members. Regardless of which management philosophy a team adopts, a lack of trust leads to anxiety, conflict, and micro-management.

Secondly, are you willing to do something every day that contributes to the success of your publication? One method I used to stay committed was to perform a task related to the magazine every single day. The task can be small, such as replying to an email, or large, such as chairing a meeting with graphic designers. Completing a task that contributes to the success of your initiative every single day will ensure that it remains high on your priority list.

Lastly, are you aware of the advantages and disadvantages your environment provides? Observe your environment and tailor your initiative to make full use of the resources available to you."

Mustafa's Job Interview Advice

"It is important to approach a job interview with the right mindset. Psychologically framing an interview as a dreaded inevitability is unhelpful. It is important to remember that giving an interview is a choice – and you must approach it in that manner. Think *"this interview is a product of my own decision to pursue this particular career at this particular firm, out of all the other paths I could have chosen"* as opposed to *"this is something I have to do but I'd rather not."* You are in control. Organisations are buyers of talent. Students should ask themselves *"can I do this job better than anyone else? Why?"* And build their preparation around that question. If you view difficult obstacles in your life as products of your own choices, you will be better equipped mentally to face them."

Successful Time Management Involves Adaptation

"Effective time management does not only involve creating a well-planned schedule but also adapting it in the face of inevitable setbacks. For example, I may have planned to complete an assessed piece of coursework and some seminar reading over a weekend, but may suddenly be faced with a printing issue for the magazine that will take a few hours to address. It is important to identify trade-offs. How important is the seminar reading relative to the coursework? How urgently does the printing issue need attention? Viewing time through the lens of opportunity cost and trade-offs can help you improve efficiency. During some hectic weeks, I would not even create set schedules – I'd set myself goals that needed to be achieved by the end of the week and improvise and adapt throughout."

Don't Just Read About Places… Go and Visit Them!

"Travelling can be a very humbling experience – especially if you visit regions that feature very different cultures and ways of life to the Western world. I was fortunate during my time as an undergraduate to travel on the Trans-Siberian Railway and visit countries such as China and Saudi Arabia. These experiences taught me valuable lessons I could not learn from simply reading about those regions in a textbook."

Live In The Moment

"Regarding regrets, I would take more time to pause and appreciate university life. I've crossed Waterloo Bridge over three hundred times in the last three years. It's a wonderful walk, especially at night. After I graduated I realised that every time I had previously walked over that bridge, I had been worried about an essay, an interview, or an exam. I never took the time to just pause, admire the view, and consider how lucky I was to be studying a subject I loved in the heart of London. It's important to live in the moment and appreciate life as an undergraduate – this period in your life will never come back!"

Growing My Vlog (Now Has Over 250,000 Subscribers) And Starting My Own Podcast

–LUCY MOON

NAME: Lucy Moon
UNIVERSITY: SOAS – University of London
DEGREE: History (BA)

Lucy Moon *(YT: Lucy Moon, IG/TW: @meowitslucy)* is a YouTube and Social Media personality with over 250,000 subscribers to her videos. Lucy regularly makes content about fashion and beauty, music, politics, self-love and university life. She is also part of the *Banging Book Club* – A fortnightly podcast that discusses books about sex and gender.

Upload Frequently

"As cliché as it has now become, the best advice I can give is to upload as frequently as possible. It pushes you to improve creatively while also playing into the website's algorithm, which favours regular uploads."

The Benefits of Extracurricular Activities

"It can be hard to commit to it when at university, but if you enjoy it then it should come as a welcome break from studying. I didn't upload for four months at a time during my second year, and it took a toll both on my channel and my productivity."

How Lucy Dealt With Anxiety In Her Second Year

"Anxiety at university was a really difficult thing for me to deal with, especially in my second year. My university had some support systems in place for those who were struggling, and so when I spoke to the student services, they were able to help. I was given some essay extensions and was able to do my exams in a special room – both solutions really helped me. When my third year came around, I made an active effort to keep on top of my deadlines from the beginning of the term, so work didn't pile up in the same way it had done. So much of my anxiety stemmed from not being sure of how much I had to do, or when my deadlines were. Buying a diary and planning my time were things I wish I had done earlier. I'd really recommend planning, organising and scheduling the things that are stressing you out – once it's on paper, it's out of your head."

What would be the one piece of advice you would give your younger self on your first day at university?

"Try not to worry about how difficult your subject is! Everyone is finding it hard, they're just better at hiding it than you are. Read a lot, and you'll be fine."

Turning Haters Into Irn-Bru Hentai Fantasisers

"Whenever I talk about social issues on my channel, I receive a barrage of comments from self-proclaimed 'meninists' who hurl abuse in my direction. I've come to see it as part of the package when you voice your opinion online, and not to take it too seriously. I try to see the funny side, and imagine most commenters as a teenage boy in his room drinking Irn-Bru and fantasising about hentai."

The Power Of The Pomodoro

"I couldn't recommend the Pomodoro technique enough! It enabled me to focus for longer periods of time and produce better work."

Having My Music Played on BBC Radio 1, Reaching The Top 40 Hip-Hop Albums on iTunes And Studying Music Technology

-JACK LIGHT

NAME: Jack Light
UNIVERSITY: Kent University
DEGREE: Music Technology (BSc)

Jack Light *(FB: @JackLightFB, Soundcloud: MCJackLight)* is a professional MC who has been featured on BBC Introducing and Channel AKA. Jack's unique lyrics vary from witty tales about his lifestyle to social commentary and has resulted in his music being played on Radio 1 and Radio 1Xtra by huge DJ's including Mary Anne Hobbs and DJ Semtex. Before arriving at university, Jack's first EP hit the top 40 in the iTunes Hip-Hop album charts within only a day of its release. His remix of Asher Roth's *Pass That Dutch* was recognised by Roth, who personally chose it as the official #1 remix, despite competition from thousands of producers around the world.

How Jack Deals With Creative Blocks

"When it comes to writer's block, I have a ridiculous number of projects on my hard drive that need working on and need completing. I know if I'm not mentally right to work on one project then there are others that I can try to work on depending on how I am feeling."

How did you manage to balance your time alongside your degree, creating music and everything else?

"I follow my diary first and the list with it. For example, I structure my days around the calendar, be it lectures, work, or social events.

Then I plan the rest of the time around the list with things such as: exercise, admin work or music. It is all about creating a balance."

If you could go back in time, what would you say to yourself at university?

"I'd say don't be too shy to get involved. Sign up to the societies and turn up to events. Don't hold back especially when asking for help – email tutors and lecturers about any problems because they are genuinely there to help and will definitely point you in the right direction. It is their job to inspire you, and that will give them satisfaction; it is a very different atmosphere to school."

What's the best book you have ever read?

"I would definitely recommend reading *Happier* by Tal Ben-Shahar. It recommends writing down five things that make you happy each day, which I incorporated into my bedtime routine. The book opened my mind to a different way of looking at life and what really makes us happy."

Setting Up A Rapidly Growing 'How To' Food Channel Teaching People To Make Tasty Meals On A Budget

–BEN LEBUS (MOB KITCHEN)

NAME: Benjamin Lebus
UNIVERSITY: University of Edinburgh
DEGREE: History (MA)

Ben Lebus is the founder of Mob Kitchen *(FB: @mobkitchen, IG: @mobkitchenuk www.mobkitchen.co.uk)*, an online publishing company producing short 'how-to' food videos. All the recipes the channel provides are 'easy to make' and 'affordable', and they pride themselves on making food 'you'll actually cook'. All the recipes require you to have is salt, pepper, olive oil and £10. Mob Kitchen's easy to follow and cheap recipes have seen them build up a large following with students and graduates alike.

The 4 Items Which The Average Student Doesn't Have But Really Should

1. "The Griddle Pan – With this you can grill meat, fish, and vegetables. I was in Tesco the other day, and it was like £11. I think everyone should definitely get one of those.

2. Microplane Grater – This is a key piece of equipment, I use a lot of chillies, and garlic and ginger and I find it tastes so much better if you grate it instead of chopping it.

3. Knife sharpener – A lot of people think they need lots of sharp knives, you don't – you just need a knife sharpener. All professional chefs never actually change the knives they use; they are just super diligent when it comes to sharpening them. You can even turn a really crappy knife into a decent one if you have a knife sharpener knocking about.

4. Colander – I like being able to steam vegetables, and if you have got a colander you don't need to get a proper steamer. You can just whack the colander over a pot of boiling water instead."

The 8 Ingredients That You Should Stock Up On At The Start Of Term

"Right at the beginning of the term, you should go to a big Tesco or Sainsbury's and stock up with the following things:

1. Sea Salt – You can get 4 boxes for a fiver, and it will last you the entire term.

2. Pepper and Olive Oil – These are the staples for any of our Mob Kitchen recipes.

3. Cumin – You can make any dish taste like you are in Morocco or Africa with a bit of cumin.

4. Smoked Paprika – This can add a Mexican vibe to any chicken and pork dishes (especially if you add the cumin in as well) – you can make some amazing fajitas and tacos.

5. Chilli Flakes – I absolutely love having chilli flakes in the kitchen. They're so versatile and can be used in so many dishes throughout term time.

6. Oregano – This is one of the best dried herbs to have and can completely transform pretty much any dish. I use this on my chicken gyros recipe which people absolutely love.

7. Coconut Milk – So useful for making any kinds of curry or soups, I fully recommend stocking up on this in bulk.

8. Apple Cider Vinegar – A good vinegar is so important. It's really good for side salads, I always found myself wishing that I had more of it at uni. You can literally liven up anything with that.

Those are all the staples and won't cost you more than £15 at the start of term."

How Mob Kitchen Got 3,000 Likes In 3 Days From A Piece Of Advice Ben Got At A House Party

"Someone came up to me at a house party, I have no memory of who it was as I had a few drinks by then but he gave me such a brilliant bit of advice… He said, *"Create Facebook groups of your friends before the launch of Mob Kitchen and give the groups special names."*

So, two weeks before the launch I made a load of Facebook groups to build up support. One group was called 'Mob Best Friends' that included all my friends from home and uni, I also had 'Mob Family' with all my cousins and other family members in it, and there was also a big group I started called 'The Mob' with over five hundred Facebook friends in. I started posting on these groups two weeks before the launch, telling them here's what I am planning on doing and here's a sneak peek of it all. The groups basically created communities of people who felt involved in what was going on. You would be absolutely amazed at the number of people who supported me right from the beginning. Even now, whenever I hit a milestone, the first thing that I do is message those groups saying thank you. I think when people start something, there's a tendency to say *"Oh I'm gonna do this thing on my own and I want all my friends to see it's become a success on its own without them having to actually help out."* Don't do that. Get your friends involved. It's unbelievable how many people feel a part of a community when they are included as part of a group. You don't have to pay them any money, just from the fact that you are an honest person who has worked hard at something and is coming to them for help. Mob Kitchen got three thousand likes in the first three days from doing this."

What's the funniest moment from your time at university?

"We always played Danger 5's with my flatmates. I remember one time at the end of term we had a load of spices that we needed to get rid of before going. So to get through them, we had a game of Danger 5's and the loser had to snort lines of garlic powder and cayenne powder!"

Creating Some Of The UK's Most Popular Fashion Blogs And Social Media Accounts And Working With Some Of The World's Largest Brands

—HANNAH LOUISE FARRINGTON, GRACE MCGOVERN & AMY LIDDELL

NAME: Hannah Louise Farrington
UNIVERSITY: University of Manchester
DEGREE: Law (LLB)

Hannah Farrington *(FB/TW/IG: @hannahlouisef, www.hannahlouisef.com)* is a blogger and social media personality. She has worked with huge brands such as L'Oreal, H&M, ASOS, Barbour, and more, as well featuring in TV campaigns for Schwarzkopf. The success of her blog led it to be shortlisted for Best Personal Style Blog in Company Magazine's style blogger awards.

NAME: Grace McGovern
UNIVERSITY: Goldsmiths University
DEGREE: Media and Sociology (BA)

Grace McGovern *(IG: @gracemcgovern, TW: @GYMCG)* is a social media personality, model signed to The Look Management and co-founder of *The G n T Blog*.

NAME: Amy Liddell
UNIVERSITY: Durham University
COURSE: Law (LLB)

Amy Liddell *(FB/TW/IG: @saltandchic, www.saltandchic.com)* is a fashion and travel blogger behind the popular blog *Salt and Chic*. Amy has worked with big brands such as Topshop, Missguided, ASOS, New Look and Lush.

Keep It Organic

Hannah – "I think that bloggers who do things like buying Instagram followers or partaking in a lot of 'like for like' culture in an unnatural way are making a mistake. That doesn't leave you with an engaged following and is annoying to genuine followers, it really limits your longevity. When I started my blog, I did not put any strategic thought into it and had no idea that blogging was a viable career for the first year or two, so I probably made every 'mistake' in the book. In spite of this, I managed to start building a following, and I imagine this is because what I was doing was natural and organic, even if it wasn't of the highest professional quality."

Get Another Person's Perspective On Your Work

Grace – "It's quite helpful having another person's thoughts, as you may think something makes way more sense in your head than it actually does. When someone else reads it they could just be like *"what on earth are you trying to say here?"* "

Make Sure You Prioritise

Amy – "When you're trying to balance a lot of things at once, it's so important to prioritise. When I had exams, for example, my blog had to take a back seat, and although I didn't have a break from blogging, I didn't post as much. It's too easy to put too much pressure on yourself, and it can be really detrimental so learning to prioritise is absolutely essential."

Hannah – "The way I managed my time was by knowing when to prioritise what. During exam periods I took a brief time off from blogging altogether, whereas over summer I would blog a lot more. I also never sacrificed my social life: for example, if I needed to get some content from a blog but also wanted to see a friend, I could ask that friend to take some photos for me before going for dinner."

Find A Niche

Grace – "I'd say you need to find a niche. Whatever your account is. That's what really brings people in, as it is those collective of groups that are drawn to others with similar tastes. As for blogging, Instagramming and what not, if you keep a consistent pattern throughout regarding colouring, size or interest that brings people in too."

Find Some 'Me Time'

Amy – "I also think that leaving some time for yourself is essential. If I just constantly work and don't have a break every now and then, whether it's a full day out or just a walk with the dogs, I start to feel sluggish, and it's really not good for your overall performance at work, university or any other tasks!"

Revision Tips From Productive Fashionistas

Hannah – "I wrote out notes in colour categories and arranged them on the walls of my flat, I did practice essays, and I recorded myself reading them to learn the facts and references they contained."

Grace – "I write up a revision plan of what theories I am going to study and for how long. Making sure to incorporate extra reading where necessary as that always gets you extra marks."

Amy – "To cope with the pressure and the workload, I created my revision notes throughout the year instead of leaving it until two months before exams, and that meant I could get stuck into the nitty-gritty of revision. I'd go home after my lectures and type up all of my lecture notes, colour code them, and then print them off to put in a display book. Although it took a lot of effort and an extra few hours of work per week, every single year when it came to exams, I thanked myself for doing it. It's also crucial to find out how you learn best. I'm a visual learner so creating colour-coded spider diagrams and notes were what really helped me."

What would be the one piece of advice you would give your younger self on your first day at university?

Hannah – "I didn't make all that much effort socially until the second half of my time at university as I had other home friends. If I were to go back, I would do more with friends from uni."

Grace – "I'd tell myself spend more time understanding my subject! It's so amazing that I was even able to go to university and I took it for granted sometimes. I wish throughout my time there, I spent more time understanding the topic rather than just learning about it."

Amy – "It would definitely be to stop being so critical of myself. I'm one of those people that constantly pick faults, whether it's with my work, my appearance or my success and I think that it added unnecessary stress to an already stressful time, especially during exams. Even though I knew I was going to be okay, I would panic every time I had a university assignment, and actually, it can end up making you perform worse than you could. I would tell myself to just try my best and whatever will be will be – if you put everything into your work, there's nothing more you can do."

Signing With Major Publishers To Get My Instagram Posts Turned Into A Memoir

—CAROLINE CALLOWAY

NAME: Caroline Calloway
UNIVERSITY: University of Cambridge
DEGREE: Art History (BA)

Caroline Calloway *(IG: @carolinecalloway TW: @carolinecalloway)* is a humorist, writer and author of the forthcoming memoir *And We Were Like.* Caroline is signed with renowned literary agent Byrd Leavell and her memoir has been sold to Penguin Random House, Macmillan Publisher and Hugo & Cie. She is also part of the Young Leader UK (YLUK) network, a network for rising stars to foster and sustain strong relations between the US and the UK.

What's the creative process behind your writing?

"This question boosts my self-esteem. This implies that I actually have a creative process! Every day I just wake up and try my best, I try and stay as happy as possible because happy is the state in which I produce my best work. I drink lots of water, exercise, I eat mostly clean but have at least one pastry to begin the day with, I talk to as many friends as possible, I do something new… and THEN I can start making my life's true calling and passion. As you can see, I am the most high maintenance person in the world. It's shocking to me that I can get anything done."

What are the biggest differences between studying in the US and the UK?

"The biggest difference in America is that you aren't an expert on America. However, in England, you do get to be an expert on

America. When people ask you questions about your country, usually things that you had no idea about, you just get to make it up. In America, I can't just be like *"It's like this, guys"* because people would be like *"No. That's not how it is!"*

Another big difference between them is the sense of humour. English people think they own sarcasm and irony. They think they have a copyright on it and that it's theirs. In America, we don't have that. We understand that they both exist equally in all countries."

Caroline's Advice To Aspiring Writers

"Define your own ideas about what is normal for a writer and what is not. Since day one, I've always thought it is so weird how everyone thinks writing is a sad career and a sad choice where you won't make any money. I simply decided from day one that I would make money and that I would be successful."

How did you manage to balance your time between your degree and your writing?

"I didn't. I decided to be a writer! I never put my degree first. It was very difficult working in the library on Instagram captions while all my other genius friends were literally inventing theories of art historical criticism. You have to follow your passion though, and I wouldn't go back and change anything."

How Caroline Met Nick (Page 256)

"There was a luncheon for Young Leaders of the UK at the US Ambassador's mansion… And I arrived about 45 minutes late! If you're invited to the young leaders' luncheon, then you shouldn't be the kind of person who'd show up to that sort of event late.

Surely those two things should somehow be self-selective? I also left my iPhone in the cab on the way there. I finally show up, and the last thing the butler says to me before he opens these bold, French double doors into the luncheon room was *"THIS SHALL NOT BE DISCREET!"* Nick was the first person I saw, I was bright red-faced sweating, and from then on we became friends."

What's the funniest moment from your time at university?

"When my best friend and I collapsed a castle while trying to break out of it (to go to a ball that we didn't have even tickets for!) The porters thought we collapsed it on purpose."

Becoming One Of The World's Most Recognisable Internet Personalities And Performing Magic At Nelson Mandela's Birthday Party

—JULIUS DEIN

NAME: Julius Dein
UNIVERSITY: Kings College London
DEGREE: International Relations (BA)

Julius Dein *(FB: @Juliusmagic, IG/TW: @JuliusDein)* is a magician, prankster, entrepreneur and one of the most recognisable online video personalities. Julius has performed at the birthday parties of Nelson Mandela and Kelly Rowland, as well as parties thrown by One Direction and Russell Brand. Julius' Facebook following grew from zero to 4,000,000 Facebook likes in one year, his online videos were viewed 500,000,000 times last year and he currently has one of the largest Snapchat followings in the UK with over 300,000 daily views. Various major news outlets such as Forbes, Business Insider, The Evening Standard, The Metro and Russia Today have all covered his work.

Being A 'Predator' And Dominating Facebook

"I decided when I got back to London (after a year abroad in LA) for my final year that I wanted to do it for myself. So I set up my own channel and worked incredibly hard. I was, and still am, what they call a 'predator' – a producer, actor, and director. I initially focused on YouTube with my content, but it wasn't actually growing at the rate I wanted as nobody saw my channel. I then started doing videos on Facebook, and they began to spread like crazy due to the share function that Facebook has. Finally, my audience started to build. It's just kept growing from there really. I made more and more videos, and it's now amazing to see how far it's come. Over ten million likes on my Facebook, verified on all my social media accounts, doing lots of brand deals with big companies. I am talking at a Snapchat conference next month about how to go viral on social media too! It's been an unbelievable journey so far."

How To Produce Viral Content (From A Guy With Over 10,000,000 Facebook Likes!)

"Good content is the primary factor in going viral. However, it's not the sole factor. It's also crucially important to make your content specifically tailored to go viral. For example, every video I make that goes online isn't going viral by luck, rest assured it's going viral by a number of different characteristics that I've specifically made and tailored to that video... I'll create a snappy introduction, a click bait thumbnail and title, and an appropriate length time too. That's just the basics; there is a whole load of other factors combined as well to produce viral content. You must also know the platform that you are using inside and out and understand how each one differs. Facebook, Snapchat, YouTube and Instagram are all unique platforms with their own pros and cons. When it comes to going viral fast, Facebook is the best platform due to the share button, which massively increases the reach of your content."

Julius On Comfort Zones

"I really don't think I am naturally more confident than other people; I just quite enjoy getting out my comfort zone. I embrace it, whether it's talking to a really attractive girl or doing some ballsy prank – I just love the buzz of getting out of my comfort zone. I think that's how I have developed my confidence. I understand what I am doing can be ridiculous, I understand that is against social norms, but I enjoy it. I've got some friends whose whole life is based on doing things outside of their comfort zone, and because of that, they are so much happier, confident, easy going and have amazing people skills. Getting out of your comfort zone is so damn underrated. It's crucial to being happy and confident in life."

The Importance Of Networking

"Whenever I go out, I will always network with the people that I meet. I will get to know them, and I will get them on Facebook. I absolutely love it. I just love meeting lots of people and making a connection with them. Doing this has led to so many opportunities! That's my one piece of advice – network."

Don't Focus On The Negativity

"I get like a hundred hateful messages a day on my social media's and emails, most of them I see what the first few letters of it are and delete them and don't respond. The way I deal with negativity is to not focus on it. I only focus on the relevant stuff. I basically ignore anything that isn't beneficial to me. The key to dealing with negativity is to just not focus on it. Focus on the positivity and the positive people. Don't dwell on the negative people because that's going to bring you down. *"Kill them with success"* – that's my motto."

Starting a Coffee Blog That Went On To Become The World's Largest Coffee Publication

–HENRY WILSON

NAME: Henry Wilson
UNIVERSITY: Durham University
DEGREE: Geography (BA)

Henry Wilson is the CEO of Perfect Daily Grind *(IG: @perfectdailygrind, www.perfectdailygrind.com)*. What started as a university student's coffee blog has now gone on to become the world's largest coffee publication and the 'go-to source for speciality coffee news and information'. Perfect Daily Grind now publishes between twenty and thirty articles per week in English and Spanish, has writers based all over the world and received between 3,000,000 and 4,500,000 views in the last twelve months.

How The World's Largest Coffee Publication Started

"I remember going to Honduras trying to learn as much about coffee as I could, and at the time, I didn't speak much Spanish. I met a coffee farmer called Oscar while I was there. He had a particularly difficult life; at the age of eleven he had to leave school, then was forced to live on his own for a period before moving in with his grandmother, and only after that did he start growing coffee. His venture wasn't particularly profitable to begin with, and he became a violent drunk, which had a particularly negative impact on his family. Oscar met someone from a local coffee cooperative, who exposed him to different processes of making coffee and it completely changed his life… He began to change the way he was growing coffee in line with these new found methods. I remember going to his farm to learn more about his method of growing coffee; he dug a hole in front of me with his hands and lifted out all these coconuts. He had realised that the hair from husks of coconuts absorbs water, so he went to the local lake, and he asked all the locals who went and drank coconut water during the summer if they could give him their empty coconut shells. They obliged, and he then proceeded to bury coffee wrapped in the coconut husks. During the dry season when the coffee was drying out, his coffee remained usable because he had the coconut hair absorb all the water in the soil and keep the coffee fresh… Upon experiencing this and returning to the UK, I realised that there was a such a disconnect between the coffee drinkers and the producers like Oscar, and I wanted to bridge that gap."

Make Your Own Coffee

"Coffee is an affordable luxury. As a student, you can't really have the best wine or the best whiskey, but for just a couple of extra pounds, you really can have the world's best coffee. I encourage students to start making coffee at home by purchasing an Aeropress. As soon as you start making your own coffee, you appreciate the subtleties of it. It's so much cheaper when you make your own coffee too, and you can have flavours from all over the world and taste all these different places."

Henry's Tip To Sourcing Ethical Coffee

"When at the point of purchase, ask yourself, *"Can I see where it has come from?"* For example, if it says the specific farm, that's great.

Traceability and accountability are directly linked. If you're just buying 'Colombian coffee', or even worse, just 'coffee', it becomes a dehumanized industry. There's no connection to where it is coming from, which means that there is no obligation to the farmer to be paid a fair price."

Henry's Travelling Advice

"Try travelling alone. Even though it's tough at times, you will get a lot more out of it and you will meet more people. Also, try and listen. A lot of people when they go travelling won't stop talking about themselves and never take the time to listen to other people. You'll learn so much more if you listen."

What would be the one piece of advice you would give your younger self on your first day at university?

"Don't be judgmental. At uni, you can make a quick judgement about someone, but then when you get to know them, it's a really different story."

What's the funniest moment from your time at university?

"In our house in the second and third year, there was this man who lived next door that decided one day he would just come round and pop in at his convenience. We were playing FIFA, and a 45-year old bloke would just knock on the door and come and sit down with us. He was a lovely guy, but he would just turn up uninvited whenever he wanted. I remember this one time when we were revising, and he was shouting up the stairs. We all tried to keep quiet because we knew if we said something that he would come up to our rooms when we were trying to revise."

Decreasing Student Failure Rate By 40%, Graduating The Top Of My Year With A Distinction In My Degree And Receiving Three Offers From Magic Circle Law Firms

—SELINA POPE

NAME: Selina Pope
UNIVERSITY: University of York
DEGREE: PPE (Philosophy, Politics and Economics) (BA)

During her studies, Selina won awards for Best Individual Academic Representative and Outstanding Contribution To Student Life, was named Achieving Excellence Scholar for her 'outstanding achievement in academic, personal and professional development' and was twice the Gold Key winner for the Scholastic Art and Writing Awards. Selina graduated top of her year with a 78% distinction in her degree, interned at Goldman Sachs and has received three offers from magic circle law firms.

How Selina Decreased Student Failure Rate By 40%

"At university, I was the department representative for my course, and I noticed over the years that the failure rate for a particular first-year maths module was very high. Over time no real solution was being found, so my friend, Beni (Page 225) and I decided to come up with a student-led solution. We sourced a group of student tutors, wrote notes and booked out teaching rooms. Students would come along, and we would go over the concepts with them in a way that broke them down into more manageable chunks. This was particularly important as most students who were failing did not do A-level maths. Following our classes, the number of students who failed decreased by 40%. The maths classes have been adopted into the department now, so we hope that, even though we have gradu-ated, students can continue to feel supported by them in the future."

Selina's Start To Finish Essay Writing Process

"The first thing I do when writing an essay is 'dissect' the question. It sounds simple but sometimes the question itself can be complicated or could have various interpretations. Once you know exactly how you're approaching it, and how you want to define ambiguous con-cepts or phrases within it, you're much better prepared to answer it. Following this, I'll spend about 80% of my time planning the essay. This is really important as a good structure and argument is key to a good mark. When planning the essay, I will be doing a lot of read-ing and research. While doing so, I will be trying to look at unique angles to approach the question from. To get a first class grade you really have to try to think out of the box. No one is expecting you to come up with a new theory or idea, but it definitely helps if, for instance, you can strongly and persuasively narrow down an answer to a particular factor, or group of factors that may not have been the most obvious or clear solution to the essay question. The biggest mistake I always used to make was to go for quantity and, thereby, sacrifice quality. It is easy sometimes to feel like you have to address all the key points you have learned about on a topic; but the most important thing is to narrow down your argument to two, maybe even one, fundamental idea. Then build the entire argument around defending and sustaining it."

Selina's CV Tips

"I would say, content aside, structure and presentation is everything. Most organisations only have around 15-20 seconds to scan over your CV before they decide which pile to put it in. Bearing this in mind, while what you have written down is crucial, the presentation of it is equally as important: you should make sure that you have chosen a clear and simple to read layout with a lot of white space included to break things up and, crucially, keep it to one page. You can find various templates online or, contact a friend who has been successful in getting an internship or job before and ask to use their template."

Selina's Best Interview Tip

"Do your research on the company, the job and, if you can, the people interviewing you. If you are asked for your opinion about that company's recent merger, and you don't know about it, it looks pretty bad."

Struggling To Manage Your Time? Write It Down

"When I had many things going on it would be easy for a couple of them to slip my mind, or for the thought of having lots to do, to overwhelm me. I found that writing everything down in clear, manageable points really helped me to understand what I needed to do and how to do it; however, it also gave me clarity when I could finally clearly see it all on a page."

Garnering Global Attention For My Extraordinary Appetite And Creating Viral Content

–KATE OVENS

NAME: Kate Ovens
UNIVERSITY: Newcastle University
DEGREE: Business Marketing and Management (BSc)

Kate Ovens *(FB: @kateovens, IG:@kate.ovens, YT: Kate Ovens)* is an influencer marketer and competitive eater. Kate has completed some of the biggest food challenges in the UK such as the 35oz Fish and Chip Challenge as well as eating a 28oz burger in under 10 minutes. Comedy Central, Mashable, HelloU and Capital FM have covered her challenges.

Kate On Going Viral On Social Media

"When starting out in social media, I read a lot about creating your own theme. However, seeing as I have different sides to my personality, that doesn't really apply to me. I just post things that I like and are relevant… In my final year, I based my whole dissertation around my Facebook page and the guerrilla marketing techniques that lead to my videos going viral on social media. I know a lot of the concepts that make certain content go viral and the underlying psychology behind it. My videos are influencer marketing that promotes restaurants and get word of mouth do all the talking rather than the traditional forced advertising. I've managed to combine my passion for marketing with my hobby and made a career out of it."

How Kate Competed In 5000+ Calorie Challenges, Lived A Student Lifestyle And Still Stayed In Shape

"I can tell you this now – it was A LOT of hard work. I went to the gym every other day while I was at university, and my diet in between challenges was a lot of protein, vegetables, fruits and good carbs. My challenges were only every three to four weeks or so – I even took a three-month gap over Christmas to revise for January exams and focus on my dissertation. My health is always my main priority. Going out with my friends may have happened once or twice a week, but it was all about balance. I think the hardest thing about staying in shape at university is the ease of just not bothering. No one is telling you that you should go to the gym or eat a healthy diet. You just want to enjoy yourself, see your friends all the time and go out. It's so easy just to pick up a meal in town rather than prepare it at home. However, the best advice I can give is to cook your own meals. Buy some Tupperware and drag it around with you. You save money, and you know exactly what goes into it. It's all about finding the right balance. Don't go too hard on the bad diet and partying lifestyle, but also don't restrict yourself so much that you don't allow for any guilty treats, foods or drinks. It's just about finding a happy medium between those two to keep everything together. During the exam period, my diet was at its best; it was the exact same thing every day just because it didn't require me to put any thought and effort into it.

Breakfast: Two egg white omelette with ham and mushrooms

Snack: Banana then later a Cheesestring

Lunch: Chicken with red onion, peppers, courgette and mushrooms

Snack: Greek yoghurt

Dinner: Salmon with broccoli

With the gym, even if you're not there for long, just get dressed and go anyway. It's better than not going in the long run. I worked out a lot at university and still do. Lots of squats, leg presses, lunges and so on. It's really not fun at all – but no pain no gain."

How Kate Deals With Negative People

"To deal with trolls, I have 3 methods:

1. Ignore them.

2. Write the reply I would love to send back (swearing and all) and then just delete it without sending.

3. Kill them with kindness."

What would be the one piece of advice you would give your younger self on your first day at university?

"Stop letting people around you think everything remotely 'out there' is cringeworthy. Just because it's not what everyone else is doing, it doesn't mean it's embarrassing. Just embrace your inner weirdness, and if people don't like it, then they aren't your real friends. Don't hold back from anything you are remotely interested in…I'm still annoyed I didn't try out for the Ice Hockey team!"

Being Crowned 'Student Reporter Of The Year' and Writing For The Guardian, The Independent, The Times, The Daily Telegraph and The Huffington Post

–HARRISON JONES

NAME: Harrison Jones
UNIVERSITY: University of Exeter (BA) and University of Sheffield (MA)
DEGREE: History and Politics (BA) and Print Journalism (MA)

Harrison Jones *(TW: @HarrisonJones7)* is an award-winning student journalist who has written for various student, national and international media outlets. During his time as editor of Exeter University's student newspaper, *Exeposé*, he saw three of his articles included in The Huffington Post's top 20 student journalist stories of the year. Harrison is also a freelance political journalist who has contributed articles to The Guardian, The Independent, The Daily Telegraph, The Times, The Huffington Post and The Egyptian Gazette. His achievements in student journalism were recognised at The Guardian Student Media Awards, where *Exeposé* was nominated for Student Publication of the Year, he was nominated for Student Feature Writer of the Year, and he won Student Reporter of the Year.

Always Get The Student Point Of View

"You have to be asking: what do students want changing at this uni? What causes do they believe in, are angered by or find interesting? Why would they read this article here when they could read it in The Guardian or The Times? That is really important for the non-news, sport or comment sections – get local or directly relevant stuff and interviews, don't rip off something that a National could have, or has, done better. Yes, there is a place for my view on the Labour crisis, but why would you read Harrison Jones when you could read Owen Jones?"[16]

People Not Taking You Seriously Can Actually Be An Advantage

"If they don't take you seriously because you're young, then it's sometimes great. I think Ed Balls, the former Shadow Chancellor, let his guard down a bit when I interviewed him. I'd planned to lull him in with the usuals and then spring this cheeky question about a weird 'love square' between him, his wife (Yvette Cooper), Ed Miliband and Stephanie Flanders (ex BBC economics editor) on him and he just did not know what to say. I think if it were an older reporter he'd have come out with "*that's not a relevant question, today we're launching X policy, blah blah blah*", but with me, he sort of looked a bit shocked and then said (of Flanders) "*dating would be overstating it.*" Which was amusing and not something you'd usually get out of a politician so high up."

Think Outside The Box

"We had to be more creative to get other stories. For example, we sent an undercover reporter with a hidden camera into an event. We told the tech company we wanted to review this piece of kit for them, which we did, but really we just wanted to use it to get the footage."

How did you go from writing for a student publication to writing for national media outlets?

"The problem for young writers, as I think I've alluded to, is that Nationals are asking the question *"why should you be writing this*

---

[16]   Owen Jones is a political journalist and author

piece?" It's all very well for you to write a great article about Jeremy Corbyn, but loads of people can do that, and most readers only want to read a select few commentators' opinion on it. So there has to be a reason why you should write this opinion piece. Now, for my first national piece, this big cheese in the coalition and the Liberal Democrats, Chris Huhne, was also my local MP and he was in the news for evading driving license points via his wife. As the editor of my college magazine, I'd interviewed him the previous year and had him on tape telling me that he was innocent. So I could use the angle *"he lied to an 18-year-old constituent's face"* as a way in to talk about why the Lib Dems, in my opinion, was losing credibility. So regarding that progression, from student publications to national outlets, you'll find most professional journalists have a background of working for 'smaller' publications where they get experience and then go to a national and say *"I should write this because I have this local experience"*, or whatever. So when I pitch to Nationals, I say *"here's my idea, here's why I should be the person to write it, and here's some of my previous work"* which back then was for smaller publications. So if you want to write for nationals, you need that grounding – it's the natural progression… When we had something potentially national newsworthy, we would forward it to the relevant people, it's so easy to find the relevant section of each paper's email address. On occasions, Nationals would find it themselves, but normally I'd recommend emailing a decent story direct to a publication(s) of choice in good time. They may even get you to write it."

Being Named 'The UK's Best Student Radio Presenter' and Now Presenting My Own Show On Absolute Radio

—SAMMY JAMES

NAME: Sammy James
UNIVERSITY: University of Leeds
DEGREE: French (BA)

Sammy James *(YT – Sammy222Fulham, www.sammyjames.co.uk)* is an award-winning radio presenter, producer and vlogger. Sammy ran a popular student radio show, which saw him crowned Best Male Presenter at the Student Radio Awards at the O2 Arena. He also created viral YouTube videos with his Taylor Swift parody *I'm Feeling a 2:2* and his rendition of *Alphabet Aerobics*. Sammy is now a producer on KISS Breakfast with Rickie, Melvin and Charlie and he also presents his own shows on the Absolute Radio Network.

Sammy On Creating Viral Content

"For me, the worst way to come up with content is to sit down and say, *"let's come up with some content"*, it's just best to let it happen naturally. That being said, what you can do is try and stay on top of what's going on in the world on TV, social media and in newspapers. That was how the *Alphabet Aerobics* video came about, as it was the day after Daniel Radcliffe did it on Jimmy Fallon's talk show. The intention was never actually to go viral, but fortunately, it piggybacked off the success of his. The *Feeling a 2:2* video was a bit more planned. It was exam season, and I saw someone post *'*I don't know about you but I'm feeling a 2:2" on Yik Yak and just thought it was a good opportunity to make the full parody video, which I hoped would be very shareable around exam time. The main thing for me is just staying on top of pop culture and consuming as much media as you can."

Create Relatable Content

"We tried to make a show with our student audience 100% in mind. This meant we would try to make as much content that was as relevant to student life as possible. Huge viral successes such as Carpool Karaoke have shown that if you can make content that is relatable to your audience's lives, (everybody's sung in a car) that it will go far."

Do you have any techniques that you use to deal with nerves and remain confident when you're performing?

"I think it's just a case of not thinking about the many people that might be listening and just imagine that you're talking to one person, which should be much less nerve-racking as most people are confident in one-to-one conversations. With nervous guests, I find it good to get them on-air as quickly as possible so that they don't have much time to think about it."

What would be the one piece of advice you would give your younger self on your first day at university?

"I think I wasn't brave enough in my first year at university when it came to the radio. It took me several months to build up the confidence to host a show, and I didn't enter any awards as I felt that it was something first years don't do. However, your time at uni is short so go for it from the start. It meant that I really had to catch-up in my final two years."

14

Athletes

"Training gives us an outlet for suppressed
energies created by stress and thus tones the
spirit just as exercise conditions the body."

–Arnold Schwarzenegger

"We must have had 99 per cent of the match,
it was the other 3 per cent that cost us."

–Ruud Gullit

Running The Final 100 Kilometres Of 'The Toughest Race On Earth' (In The Sahara Desert!) With A Broken Leg

–JAMES TUFNELL

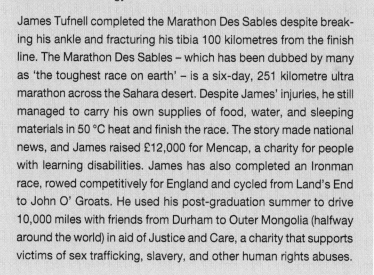

NAME: James Tufnell
UNIVERSITY: Durham University (BA) and University of
Cambridge (MSc)
DEGREE: Archaeology

James Tufnell completed the Marathon Des Sables despite breaking his ankle and fracturing his tibia 100 kilometres from the finish line. The Marathon Des Sables – which has been dubbed by many as 'the toughest race on earth' – is a six-day, 251 kilometre ultra marathon across the Sahara desert. Despite James' injuries, he still managed to carry his own supplies of food, water, and sleeping materials in 50 °C heat and finish the race. The story made national news, and James raised £12,000 for Mencap, a charity for people with learning disabilities. James has also completed an Ironman race, rowed competitively for England and cycled from Land's End to John O' Groats. He used his post-graduation summer to drive 10,000 miles with friends from Durham to Outer Mongolia (halfway around the world) in aid of Justice and Care, a charity that supports victims of sex trafficking, slavery, and other human rights abuses.

As With Many A Great Story – It Started With A Bet In The Pub

"I had heard that my boss had recently done an Ironman [challenge] and was planning to take part in the Marathon des Sables. Over lunch, I did some research on it, and when I arrived at the pub to meet some school friends; I mentioned to them that I was thinking about taking part that year. Given that I am 6 foot 2, fair-skinned, ginger-haired, and notoriously bad at cross-country running, you can imagine how funny they found this. One of my friends who knows me the best was apprehensive about how I would deal with my other friends' reactions. He knew that I have the tendency to want to prove people wrong when challenged, and he seriously warned me against it for the sake of my own health. Despite this, I – in what I can only describe as a youthful and farcical manner – decided to bet the next round of drinks that I could, in fact, do it. I promptly signed up on my phone while one of my friends bought a round of drinks. It is one of the wonders and terrors of the modern age that you can sign up to something quite so completely insane so easily in such a short space of time."

The Injury

"My injury occurred on the morning of the fourth day, 5 miles into a 60-mile day. Having started the day with the organisers blaring AC/DC's *Highway to Hell* at full volume from a helicopter, we were sent up what is best described as a sand mountain. On the way down the sandy descent, while planting my heels to stop myself toppling over as happened to one competitor, I jarred the heel of my ankle hard on the point of a rock hidden in the sand. When I was at school, I had broken my ankle playing rugby, and the break essentially looked like my ankle had exploded like a hand grenade with bits of bone everywhere. I thought it had healed fine, but this moment three years later proved otherwise as essentially the exact same thing happened!"

Chocolate + Painkillers + A Refusal To Fail + Avril Lavigne = James's Desert Survival Pack

"After about twenty-five miles of walking in immense agony and having cried my eyes out reading a letter that one of my housemates had written me, I was seriously questioning my ability to finish the next sixty miles. I arrived exhausted at the halfway checkpoint and realised I was left with two options. Firstly, drop out and let the pain of defeat sink in, resigning myself to failure and a depressing ride on a quad bike for thirty miles to the rug held up by sticks which quantified itself as my tent. Or basically, having some painkillers, a piece of chocolate, putting on my *Feel Good* shuffle playlist and sucking it up and dealing with it. Being unable to face flying home to the jeers of friends and inevitably buying an expensive round of London-priced drinks, I chose the latter.

My brain works in such a way that I thought if I failed it there and then, I would have to come back next year. I realised that simply finishing the race and never coming back was the way I would have the shortest time in the desert, and so the best thing to do was just to carry on!

I marched up to the doctor at the checkpoint and pleaded for the strongest painkillers he had. He promptly, but somewhat reluctantly gave them to me, with the passing comment in French of, *"you English fool, this race isn't everything, you all sometimes need to know when to give up"* along with an injection to help thin my blood to stop a blood clot going up from my swollen ankle to my brain and giving me a stroke. The next thirty miles I honestly cannot remember very much of, apart from that I listened to a lot of Taylor Swift and learnt all the words to Avril Lavigne's *Sk8r Boi,* such was my delirium. The other competitors and I were like empty shells of people; there was nobody at home. Just bodies with shrunken eyes, moving silently and solemnly like pilgrims towards the day's finish line. Nobody spoke to each other as we wandered like a bunch of fireflies towards the glow sticks that marked our route. Fortunately, the painkillers worked, and after about ten miles of horrid, unfathomable pain, my ankle went completely numb and I was able to put some more weight on it. Moreover, much to the detriment of my recovery, I actually started to run again. I finished the stage at about 2 AM."

Overtaking A Childhood Hero

"The last day of the marathon was conclusively the hardest day of my life. The dropout pace of the Marathon des Sables is set by a series of very slow camels. If you fall behind the camels, you are disqualified. With the camels within arm's reach almost immediately I realised I had to muster up some strength from somewhere to go a bit faster. I cracked on at a better pace and then had my first interaction of the day with one of my childhood heroes, Sir Ranulph Fiennes, as he was in and amongst a group of runners. I had met him earlier in the week because I was the youngest Briton in the race and he was the oldest. As I passed him I looked over and said, "*Sir Ranulph – from the youngest Briton to the oldest, in the immortal words of Sir Winston Churchill, 'Keep buggering on!'*" I finished the race by myself and nearly collapsed on the finish line after an eleven-hour and thirty-minute marathon. I did not see Sir Ranulph again until that evening, where we saw each other in the medical tent. The magnitude of how special that day was did not sink in for a while. I had just completed the toughest race on the planet, as the youngest European entrant, somehow won my age category through the shift I had put in earlier in the race; and done so with one of my childhood heroes, the world's greatest explorer."

The Shoes Choose The Runner

"Buy a decent pair of trainers and choose them based on how they feel, not on the advertising. Think of the Harry Potter wand mantra, because the trainer really does choose the runner. When you try on the right pair of trainers you just know; they fit well, are comfortable, and feel like you're wearing a sock."

What would be the one piece of advice you would give your younger self on your first day at university?

"Never believe a prediction that doesn't empower you, and don't let fear rule you. I have learnt that advice is a very difficult and dangerous thing to give out, and I try to steer towards offering encouragement rather than advice. I am a firm believer that the best thing to advise oneself is one's own subconscious and to listen to what it has to say. There will always be obstacles, moments where you want to pack it in, issues of self-doubt, but if you use the ultimate human super power available to us all, intelligent reasoning and rational thinking you can achieve things you cannot comprehend. Confucius said *"He who says he can and he who says he can't are both usually right"*. Think through the problems or goals you have reasonably, don't let fear govern your actions, back yourself and you will be amazed at what you can achieve."

Going From Being An Unhealthy Student To A Personal Trainer and Recognised Social Media Personality (Now An Adidas Global Ambassador And Amazon Best-Selling Author)

–ZANNA VAN DIJK

NAME: Zanna van Dijk
UNIVERSITY: University of Sheffield
DEGREE: Speech and Language Therapy (BSc)

Zanna van Dijk *(IG/FB/TW: @zannavandijk, www.zannavandijk. co.uk)* is a personal trainer and health, fitness and travel social media personality and blogger. Zanna is also an author, with her book *Strong* making it to Amazon's Top 100 books. Zanna has built a substantial following online that has allowed her to travel and work with a variety of brands and is currently signed as an Adidas Global Ambassador. Her success has led her to be on the front cover of The Sunday Times Style and Women's Fitness.

Zanna's Student Fitness Beginnings

"I was a typical unhealthy student, living a life full of ready meals and boozy nights out. I started to feel tired, lethargic and basically unhealthy. I was sluggish and found it to be hard to concentrate, plus I wasn't happy with how my skin was deteriorating and developing acne. I looked to fitness and nutrition as a way to boost my energy and brainpower, clean up my skin and improve my overall health. In between my studying, I spent my time reading about the topics and getting nerdy. My interest in fitness soon went from a hobby to a passion and as a result I setup my blog and social media accounts on the topic. The rest is history, as they say."

From your experience, what do you see as the main causes of weight gain at university for most students?

"Being thrust into a new situation and often not knowing how to cook nutritious meals can mean you turn to takeaways. Boozy nights out can total up to thousands and thousands of calories, not to mention the kebab you grab on the way home. Students often unknowingly increase their caloric intake significantly and reduce the quality of their food choices. The best way to stay on track at uni is to rein in your diet, then look to exercise. Develop an awareness of what you're putting into your body and try not to consume food and drinks in excess. Stay active and rope your friends and flatmates into cooking healthy meals or going on runs together."

Zanna's Diet And Workout Schedule

"My diet varies every single day. I don't track my macronutrients or caloric intake as I am very in tune with my body, so I intuitively eat. I try to eat a balanced diet that contains enough lean protein. I also follow the '80/20 rule', which means I eat healthy, nourishing foods 80% of the time and less nutritious meals or treats 20% of the time. Nothing is off limits. Everything in moderation! An example day would look like this:

Breakfast: Oats with protein powder, fruit and peanut butter.

Lunch: An omelette packed with veggies and topped with cheese e.g. feta.

Snack: An apple with cinnamon.

Dinner: Salmon, sweet potato and veggies.

Dessert: Yoghurt with chocolate chips, strawberries and cashews.

At university, I was training 4-5 times a week. I was doing purely weighted workouts using dumbbells, barbells and cables. I have since moved onto a more varied training program and now mix resistance training 3-4 times a week with HIIT sessions 1-2 times a week. My favourite exercises are hip thrusts and deadlifts (for the posterior chain) and also pull ups."

Motivation Through Scheduling

"My favourite way to keep myself motivated is scheduling. I schedule in my workouts like they are doctors appointments – I can't cancel them. I literally plan the rest of my working day around them as much as I can. I also use spreadsheets to structure my workouts for the following two weeks, to ensure I am getting to the gym enough and maintaining a balanced regime. However, ultimately motivation comes from within. Once you get into a rhythm with your training, you won't want to stop. I promise!

I am by nature one of the most organised, scheduled and regimented people you will probably ever meet. I live my life by to-do lists and time management is my forte. The main way I fitted everything in was through scheduling. I would look to the hours, days or weeks ahead and literally plan things down to the minute to ensure everything was done on time."

What's your biggest regret about your time at university?

"I would have established a better work-life balance. My degree was four years long, and in my first three years I literally ran myself into the ground in an attempt to get the best marks possible; and sacrificed my personal life to do so. However, in my fourth year, I realised that I didn't have to spend every waking moment in the library to do well, and actually giving yourself time off allows you to work more efficiently. I wish I had realised that earlier on."

Overcoming Depression and Becoming the UK's Smallest Bodybuilder

–CHOON TAN

NAME: Choon Tan
UNIVERSITY: Northumbria University
DEGREE: Applied Sports & Exercise Science (BSc)

Choon Tan (IG: @imchoontan) is the UK's smallest bodybuilder. Choon found out at the age of thirteen that he has an incredibly rare genetic birth defect called x-linked spondyloepiphyseal dysplasia tarda that impairs bone growth, causes back pain and other physical complications. The condition affects only 1 in 500,000 people. He was regularly bullied as a child and experienced bouts of depression as a result. He overcame his depression through bodybuilding and self-development. Choon is also a UKBFF sponsored athlete and well-known personality.

Choon's Story

"I was most depressed at the age of fifteen, and I didn't have the will to live anymore. I would go to bed crying every night wanting everything to end. It had all gotten to me, from the bullying at school, to problems at home and struggling with this genetic defect. I felt like I didn't have a purpose in life and that there was nothing to hold onto."

Create A Positive Lifestyle

"When people are depressed, it is either physiological, psychological or both. So you'll want to do things to alleviate both. Create a way of life that you are happy to live, with a healthy diet and exercise to ensure that your brain is producing the right hormones. And surround yourself with positive people who will motivate and inspire you."

Take Action

"My philosophy is to be friendly with everyone and to try and make everyone laugh or smile if possible. I always try to look for the positive in a situation. If a girl rejects me, oh well, at least I've taken action and learnt something from it. I firmly believe taking action is the one thing that gives you a positive outlook on life, as it gives you the feeling of control over your life and your mind."

Choon's Guide To Becoming The Best Version Of Yourself

"Self-development is about striving to become the best version of yourself: Physiologically, psychologically and spiritually. Learning how to be your own best friend is fundamental because you either control your brain, or it controls you. Ultimately the goal is to create a more meaningful and positive life for yourself where opportunities and relationships are in abundance. Meditation and bioenergetics have substantially boosted my social confidence and skills.

Meditation allows me to clear my mind of all thoughts (especially negative ones). Through this, I have alleviated a lot of my depression and almost all of my anxiety as it helps you to access repressed emotions and the breathing exercises release more endorphins. Meditation also trains your brain to work at a higher capacity and engages with flow states more, so during social situations you will be more engaged and have significantly improved social awareness.

Bioenergetics is about releasing neurotic holding patterns and any tension held in the body. It runs around the concept that the mind will follow the body and the body will follow the mind. So it involves a lot of shaking of the body, deep breathing and screaming as loud as possible. This will train your brain to realise that you can be as loud as you want in an environment and nothing bad will happen. This will make your voice and the way you speak much more prominent in social situations. (Check out Elliott Hulse's videos on Bioenergetics)."

Choon's 9 Rules For A Happy And Confident Life

1. Meet as many new people as you can.

2. Try to break a comfort zone daily.

3. Say yes to as many opportunities as you can.

4. In 100 years everything you know and everyone you know will be gone, so what does it matter if you embarrass yourself, get rejected or fail now? The only failure is not trying.

5. Start a conversation with someone you find attractive every day (if you're single!)

6. Join as many clubs and societies as possible.

7. Exercise every day.

8. Avoid negative people.

9. Try transcendental meditation every day.

Choon's Workout Advice

"The exercises that I recommend for getting in shape are deadlifts, handstand push ups, leg press, squats, bench press, dumbbell press, pull-ups and dips."

Choon's Ninja Experience

"The best experience I've had however was competing on Ninja Warrior UK recently. It was by far the best day of my life and the biggest challenge I have ever undertaken."

What's the best book you have ever read?

"*The Power of Now* by Eckhart Tolle is without a doubt the best book I have ever read. The book describes where fear and anxiety originate from and how to manage negative and useless thoughts. The book can basically help you to become a more conscious human being and teaches you how to live life without being too affected by negative things that are out of your control."

Life As Gymshark Athletes, Fitness Moguls And Successful Personal Trainers

-LEX AND LAINEY GRIFFIN

NAME: Alexander 'Lex' Griffin
UNIVERSITY: Newcastle University
DEGREE: Biology (BSc)

Lex Griffin *(IG:@lex_fitness, TW: @Lexonidas, YT: Lex Fitness)* is a fitness model, Gymshark sponsored athlete and personal trainer. Lex has competed on stage in bodybuilding competitions, featured on the cover of Men's Health and was also a mixed martial artist before coming onto the fitness scene.

NAME: Lainey Griffin
UNIVERSITY: Dublin Institute of Technology[17]
DEGREE: Biomedical Sciences (BSc)

Lainey Griffin *(IG: @laineybopster, TW: @LAINEYBOPSTER, YT: Lainey Griffin)* is an online diet coach, Gymshark sponsored athlete and personal trainer. Lainey has competed on stage in bikini competitions and previously worked in a blood transfusion lab.

What are the biggest mistakes you've seen with students and their training?

Lex – "Not taking advantage of university facilities… There won't be a time where the gym is cheaper or more accessible, and you'll never have more time to train than when you're at uni. I know people think that they have loads of work at uni, but when you get out into the real world, you realise how much free time you actually had when

---

[17] We are aware that Lainey didn't go to university in the UK but her insight was too good to let geography ruin it.

you were there! I think another big thing is that at uni it's most likely the first time you start training properly. A lot of people start the gym and immediately start using supplements and rely on them from the get-go, instead of making sure their diet is in check – I know that's what I did, my friends and I were on Creatine right from the start! I think especially with a student budget, get your diet right first, and then look to supplementation as a secondary issue."

Use Your Uni Timetable

Lainey – "At uni, they literally give you a timetable. You know when all your lectures and seminars are, so put the gym in there too! If I could go back to uni and do it all again, I would block off my time; if I knew I had three hours off before lectures, I would timetable the gym into that gap. The gym is going to energise you, so use that schedule to work in your workouts. Be reasonable with yourself too; if you know you have nine hours of lectures one day, you're going to be knackered, and you're probably not going to be able to fit in a session that day. But the day you've got an hour of lectures, you can go and do a tough session, and you'll know that you've used your time most effectively."

Try Everything As A Student, Not Just The Gym

Lainey – "Going to the gym at uni is more about feeling good and being healthy. Use the gym to burn off the kebab you ate last night rather than being so focused on just lifting weights or becoming a bodybuilder or whatever. There are so many clubs at uni to get involved with. There are experts who'll teach you, everything from rock-climbing to beginners' rugby. There are so many opportunities at university. It's your chance to experiment, if you don't like it, don't do it! Just try as much as you can."

Lex and Lainey's Student Home Gym Recommendations

Lex – "My top three would be a pull-up bar, kettlebells, and a floor mat. Kettlebells are fantastic, they're functional, and you can do every part of your body with them. A pull-up bar is so cheap, they won't damage a student house, and they're great for building strength."

Lainey – "Resistance bands. Definitely. You can take them on holiday, take them out wherever you want, and you can do your whole body with them. Even in an entirely empty room you can do push ups, sit ups, etc. so there's no reason to miss a workout."

Eating Healthy Food Doesn't Equate To A Balanced Diet

Lainey – "The main thing I find, especially with girls who are into fitness and the gym, is that a lot of them who say *"I'm not growing a bum, or getting abs"* and my response is always *"so… what's your diet like?"* to which they reply, *"Oh I'm eating healthily."* Nutrition isn't something that boils down to just 'eating healthily' – a bag of nuts is "healthy", it's organic, and it's good for you – but it's a bag of fat! You need to balance it with a good amount of protein and carbs and make sure that you're eating a well-rounded, balanced diet. On the other side of that, there are girls who are just not eating and putting pressure on themselves, which leads to eating disorders. Your diet is crucial to success, regardless of what you're doing, whether it's a sport, just going running or going to the gym, you need to make sure you're getting the right nutrients. Loosely track your food intake, and you'll be able to see where you're at. There's so much information out there on diet and nutrition on YouTube, so go out and read and listen to as much as you can."

Make The Liquor Fit Your Macros

Lex – "Drinking is a major factor to consider. Everyone's going to go out and party, you're at uni and it's one of the most sociable times of your life. So, because alcohol is essentially macronutrient in and of itself, make sure you factor that in. A really easy tip is to ensure you don't eat when you're out, so eat beforehand, it'll prevent you putting on a load of weight! Also if you've had a heavy night, control your calorie intake the next day, and make sure you eat later on that day, after the alcohol has left your system – because alcohol takes precedent in the body when it comes to digestion. If you do have to eat when you're out, skip the cheesy chips, and go for a grilled chicken pita."

Half Time Night Club Breaks For A Panini

Lainey – "I was awful with eating when I was out! I was renowned for being a mid-night out eater, the bouncers knew what I was like, I'd go out for a panini in the middle of a night out, and they'd see me and know that I'd be back in after I'd eaten!"

What would be the one piece of advice you would give your younger self on your first day at university?

Lex – "Actually go to the library! I turned up to the library with my best mate on the first day of my second year and couldn't get in as my card didn't work because I hadn't set foot in the library at all the previous year. When we went to reception to ask to be let in, the lady just *"aww'd"* at us, assuming we were freshers; we grinned and to her horror replied: *"Nope, we've done a year already!"*"

Lainey – "Like yourself first. I always took myself really seriously, and I judged myself a lot, I was focused on people liking me rather than actually liking myself. I think a lot of people are focused on other people liking them, rather than actually liking themselves. You can become a person that you're not, and it's not about being cocky or arrogant, but being confident in your views, yourself and what you believe in."

Balancing Seven Sports Alongside My Degree And Preparing For The Tokyo 2020 Olympics

—MORGAN LAKE

NAME: Morgan Lake
UNIVERSITY: Loughborough University
DEGREE: Psychology (BSc)

Morgan Lake *(TW: @morgan_a_lake, IG: @morganalexandralake)* is a Team GB track and field athlete. She holds six UK age group records, twenty-three national age group titles and was the world's best Under-18 heptathlete and high jumper. At Rio 2016, she became the first British woman to reach an Olympic high jump final since 1992. Morgan is also an official Nike UK and Red Bull athlete who is now training for the Tokyo 2020 Olympics.

The Power Of The List

"Trying to balance seven sports alongside a degree is difficult, but I'm managing. I'm very much a list person. I know what I am doing each slot of the day. I don't always stick to it exactly, but I just like knowing where and when I am going to be throughout the day."

Yoga For The Flow State

"I do a lot of yoga. It helps with calmness; I usually do that before a competition when I am feeling nervous. It really helps with my mindset and gets me into a flow state. It's brilliant for clearing the mind."

Morgan On Setting Goals

"I like having a long-term goal. It's a way of motivating myself in training knowing what I'm working for. Then I set short-term goals too. I like having things immediately in the future that I can focus on, the short-term goals are just loads of little stepping stones towards that big goal."

Early To Rise

"I do really like getting up early. I like having enough time in the morning to chill, have a coffee and make my breakfast. I like having a period in the morning where I can relax instead of sleep in and then have to rush!"

Always Check The Dress Code

"It was the closing night of the competition [European Junior Championship], and there was a banquet that evening. Just beforehand, we had a full team meeting to debrief everyone about the championship; the coaches and the team directors were all there. A friend and I thought everyone was getting ready for the banquet before the team meeting… So, we turned up to this meeting ready to go out, but when we arrived, everyone was looking really serious in full kit. We had to sit there, ready to party while everyone was having a serious meeting about the competition. Not ideal!"

Running A Combined 2,600 Miles In 100 Continuous Marathon Relays With My Teammates (Breaking The Current World Record By 757 Miles!) And Raising Half A Million Pounds For 'Brain Tumour UK' In The Process

−ANTHONY MEENAGHAN

NAME: Anthony Meenaghan
UNIVERSITY: Sheffield Hallam University
DEGREE: Architectural Technology (BSc)

Anthony Meenaghan was part of a team who ran 2,600 miles in one hundred continuous marathon relay stages around the UK. They beat the current world record by 757 miles in an attempt to raise £500,000 for Brain Tumour UK. Anthony received the baton twice during the eighteen-day challenge running the equivalent of two marathons within ten days. During the world record attempt, he was also part of the support crew that accompanied the runners at each stage, meaning he ran over one hundred miles throughout the challenge. Anthony regularly runs for charities and has been part of a twenty-hour ultramarathon in America and raised £25,000 for Multiple Sclerosis.

Anthony's Motivation

"I believe it's important in life to give back and make a difference. I'm grateful for everything I have in my life, family, friends, my health and my education. For me, it's personal motivation to run and raise money for good causes. To know that I'm helping fund research and that one day the cure for cancer will be found – that's what keeps me going. I highly recommend students taking part in charitable activities during university, there are so many things you learn as a person going the extra mile to help others and make a positive difference."

Anthony's Running Tips

"Set a realistic goal and enjoy the experience of running and having fun, that's what it's all about. When it comes to raising money, the best avenue to get donations from is through networking. Your university, local newspapers, radio, and the power of social media can help spread the word all over the world… Energy gels and music are essential when you're out running for a long time. The gels and a song with a fast beat help keep the energy levels up!"

What's your biggest regret about your time at university?

"I should have asked more questions. I was embarrassed at times to ask for help or advice in front of the class when I didn't understand something. Looking back I wish I took advantage more of the experienced lecturers who had the knowledge and expertise that would have benefitted my learning."

Developing A Passion For Fitness In My Erasmus Year And Becoming 'The UK's Most Followed Law Student'

−SAFFRON SHERIFF

NAME: Saffron Sheriff
UNIVERSITY: Lancaster University, Universitat Konstanz, University of York and BPP Manchester
DEGREE: Politics with International Relations (Foundation Year) LLB Law (Undergraduate Degree) Political Science (Erasmus Year) LPC at BPP (Postgraduate Degree)

Saffron Sheriff *(IG/TW/FB: @SaffronSheriff)* is an internet fitness personality who started pursuing fitness at university during her Erasmus year. She has been labelled in the media as 'The UK's Most Followed Law Student'.

Avoid Health Extremes At Uni

"The best advice I could ever give to people is 'don't be extreme'. Having an extremely unhealthy lifestyle will make you sick, but so will being obsessively healthy. There is so much misinformation about weight loss; you don't need to exercise to lose weight, just eat healthily. Equally, you can't outrun a bad diet. Extreme diets lead to extreme binges, I've seen people go on crazy 1200 calorie diets, end up bingeing out of starvation, then beating themselves up for not being able to stick to an impossible diet. I've also seen people binge day in and day out and then force themselves to exercise to a point where they clearly aren't enjoying themselves. Doing things like this will ruin your mental health and your grades. Focus on your daily healthy habits instead and look for healthier alternatives that you will stick to. Most importantly remember that your degree is the most important thing at this point in your life, and not that little bit of fresher or Christmas weight."

Always Take Both Sides On Board

"Listen to the people who encourage you, respect the opinions of those who don't and don't be defensive when people offer you advice. You need a certain level of confidence to stand up and say, *"This is who I am, and this is what I am doing"*. Without this, you won't last long against criticism."

Saffron's Take On Studying Abroad

"It was very eye opening. I'd never been abroad in my entire life before my Erasmus year. I'll never forget the day I got on a plane, arriving at my empty flat at 2 AM, sleeping on a mattress using a coat as a duvet cover. It was incredible; I was so excited. I never had any doubts about what I was doing. I think I was too curious for my own good sometimes. I ended up befriending another foreign girl from Ukraine on a skiing trip who turned out to be my next-door neighbour. We used to get up at 5 AM every morning, I would knock on her front door with a cup of coffee ready, and she would sit in the basket of my bicycle, and I would cycle us up to the gym. We would go to uni, spend all afternoon swimming in the lake and she would give me German lessons at night. In summer, we would carry a giant barbell to the meadow behind our flat and practice deadlifting. In winter, we would spend all weekend skiing in Switzerland… I dragged her into so much trouble all the time. I remember us climbing a zoo gate, ditching our university group to break into a castle or finding ourselves inside abandoned hospitals at 11 PM. Living in Germany has given me so many memories that I still find myself laughing at even now."

The UK's Most Accomplished BUCS (British University and College Sport) Athletes (The UK Boxing Champion And The Captain of The UK's Most Successful Uni Football Team)

–DANNY HIRST & SAM MINIHAN

NAME: Danny Hirst
UNIVERSITY: Manchester Metropolitan University
DEGREE: International Business (BA)

Danny Hirst *(TW/IG: @DannyJHirst)* was a sports scholar at Manchester Metropolitan University and was crowned the BUCS boxing champion in the 60-64KG division. Danny won gold after beating University of West England's Rahim Nanji in the final via split decision.

NAME: Sam Minihan
UNIVERSITY: Loughborough University
DEGREE: Sport and Exercise Science (BSc)

Sam Minihan was the captain of the UK's most successful university football team – Loughborough University Football Club. Loughborough has been UK BUCS champions 35 times in its history, which is more than any other university football team in the UK. Sam captained his team in BUCS, the FA Cup, and the FA Vase as well as against Manchester United's Under 18's.

Individual Sports Vs. Team Sports At University

Danny – "Motivation in individual sports has to be one of the hardest things to conquer, as it's very different from having a team around you who are all working towards the same collaborative goal. When it's just you, there are many nights when you're running late at night by yourself or just hitting a bag. The hardest time to find motivation in an individual sport like boxing is when you lose. There are occasions where you will sit back afterwards and get angry about all the work you put in just to have lost!

The way that I kept motivated was by telling myself what I'm doing it for. I would remind myself that boxing was keeping me fit, it was helping my brain function at university but most of all it was giving me unrivalled satisfaction after a hard session."

Sam – "With a team sport you've got to have three things – ambition, loyalty, and trust. Also, I think it is crucial to have an understanding of your teammates as each player is there for a different reason. As a captain of a team, you have to understand all of this and motivate the group."

Staying Relaxed Under Pressure

Danny – "The general protocol we were taught in our gym was to "*train every day as if you're fighting tomorrow*". Another thing I found when I was about twenty was that listening to music to get me in the zone never actually worked. I found I depended on the music being there to get pumped up. So instead, I decided to get ready about two hours before my fight and go outside the venue, rain or shine, and just do shadow boxing and stretching warm ups, this meant that I could relax and avoid getting too hyped up."

The Importance Of Sport's Socials And How To Throw A Great House Party

Sam – "I found that the best opportunity to bond as a team was Wednesday night BUCS sports socials, perhaps due to the influence of alcohol which tended to encourage individuals to open up a little more…(Regarding Sam's house that got labelled 'Loughborough's most notorious party house' by the press) The location of the house is crucial, as my house later discovered, so aim to find a spot surrounded by students. I must also add having access to a dartboard, chocolate cake, suitcases and trampolines is a recipe for disaster, and so should be avoided at all costs! Trust me on that one."

What's the funniest moment from your time at university?

Danny – "It's hard to pick one and even more difficult to choose one suitable for the public! But I guess they always revolved around nights out. I always had a habit of sleepwalking after a night out, so it always ended up with me wandering around in student halls and waking up on the bathroom floor the next day!"

Sam – "Following a night out we decided for some reason that it would be a good idea to toboggan down our staircase on suitcases using a colander as a helmet. The next morning we found out it had gone viral on social media."

Overcoming Chronic Fatigue, Finishing Second In The World At The Red Bull Street Style Championships, Working With Brands From Nike to Coca-Cola and Producing Music For The World's Biggest Vloggers

–DANIEL DENNEHY

NAME: Daniel Dennehy
UNIVERSITY: Dublin City University[18]
DEGREE: Media And Communications (BA)

Daniel Dennehy *(IG: @danielgothits)* is a football freestyler, music producer and rapper. Daniel's battle to overcome chronic fatigue and become the runner up at the Red Bull Football Freestyle World Championship in Rome was the subject of the documentary *GENK UP*. His freestyling ability has led him to star in global campaigns for brands such as Nike, Coca-Cola and Adidas. His music has also been used by vloggers all over the world including Casey Neistat and Gary Vaynerchuk.

Dan's Battle With A Fungus That Led Him To An 85-Year-old Mozart Loving Brazilian Doctor

"At uni, I was constantly coming home more and more tired. I didn't feel right inside myself. It was so weird. I kept visiting doctors, and they couldn't figure out what was wrong with me. They got me to do blood tests, STD tests, I did everything, and they still didn't know what it was. So I started googling it, and I found about a fungus called Candida; it takes all the nutrients out of your body, it can make you feel depressed, dizzy, blurred vision and out of body

---

[18] We are aware that Lainey didn't go to university in the UK but her insight was too good to let geography ruin it.

feelings. It described exactly what I had, and I was convinced it was what I had. I wanted to get tested for it, but the doctors said there was no chance I had candida. They said it would be impossible. Literally, every doctor I visited said it wasn't candida. In a last ditch attempt, I flew to Brazil (where my mum is from) and visited a specialist out there. He was a gastroenterology specialist, who only deals with stomach and intestine problems, he was like eighty-five years old, and I remember him constantly listening to Mozart. He checked my intestines and eventually told me *"you have a lot of candida in there!"* I just burst out crying with my mum. I was so happy that I finally knew what was wrong. Now I could get it fixed and get my health back to normal. In a way I am grateful it happened, it's made me appreciate the value of health for the rest of my life."

Dan's Recovery From Hospital Bed To Runner-Up At The World Championships

"After recovering from the candida, I just wanted to get back training and get healthy. After five weeks of training, I got back to my previous level. At that point, I was really motivated for the World Championships. I started training six hours a day for seven to eight months in a row. I ended up going from being ill to finishing second in the World Championships. It was an amazing feeling. I remember people coming up to me telling me to not cry because second place was amazing. I wasn't crying because I was sad at the fact I lost, I was crying because of how happy I was and how far I had come."

Long Term Success Starts With Just A Single Successful Day

"If you have a successful day today, and you do that seven days in a row, then you've had a successful week. If you do that four weeks in a row, then you had a successful month. If you do that for twelve months in a row, then you had a successful year. It all starts with having a successful day. I think the highest achieving people make sure every day something is accomplished. Every day I ask myself, *"what do I need to do today to make today a success?"*

How Dan Went From Making Beats In His Room To Getting Air Time On The Some Of The World's Biggest Vlogs

"I was looking at one of his (Casey Neistat) first vlogs, in the corner of his screen you could see a tab open on his laptop, and I could just make out his email! I sent him an email saying, *"Hey Casey, I'm a producer... I would love to send you some of my beats."* That's the key, I didn't send them, I just asked – *"is there any way I could email you my three coolest beats, and if you like them you can use them?"* – I made it really easy for him to reply to it and he did, he said *"Yeah sure."* The next thing I did was change the name of the beat. Instead of just emailing him 'Beat #1' – I named the beat something specifically related to him. He had a company at the time called Beme, so I called it 'Beme Boyz.' He liked it and he started using it and started tagging my name in his vlogs. As soon as Casey started using my music, it then opened up the door to so many other vloggers around the world who started using my beats too."

Overcoming Adversity, Being Undefeated At The Olympics And Winning A Gold Medal

–LILY OWSLEY

NAME: Lily Owsley
UNIVERSITY: University of Birmingham
DEGREE: Sports, Exercise and Rehabilitation (BSc)

Lily Owsley MBE was an ever-present member of the undefeated GB hockey team that won gold at the 2016 Rio Olympics. Lily scored in the final that finished 3-3 and Team GB went on to beat the current world champions Holland on penalties. Lily and her teammates were all named on the New Years Honours list for their remarkable achievements at the Olympic Games where they won all eight of their matches and over nine million people tuned in to watch their final game. The International Hockey Federation also recently awarded Lily with the World Hockey's Rising Star of the Year award.

How Team GB Responded To Failure

"We put two years training into it (The Hockey World Cup), and we ended up finishing eleventh. It was catastrophic. We knew as a team something had to change after that. We sat down together after the tournament and decided that fundamentally, it was our culture that we needed to sort out. And before we thought about getting back on the training pitch, we sat through hours and hours of meetings laying out our new culture. We asked ourselves what we wanted to represent and what are our vision, values and behaviours were. We decided from these meetings that we wanted to 'be the difference, create history and inspire the future'. From this, we then had a list of vision, values and behaviours that we could do individually and collectively every single day."

What Some See As Adversity, Others See As Challenges

"Unfortunately for me, just two months before the Olympic qualifiers, I contracted meningitis. Safe to say this was not where I wanted to be two months from an Olympic qualifier! However, as soon as I left the hospital and I had some love from my mum back at home, I headed straight back into training to go through rehab to get back to peak fitness.

Luckily, my coach had faith in me that I was going to deliver. I got back to full health, got through the tournament, and we ended up winning the European Championships that summer. We kept on winning and winning; our baseline kept getting higher and higher. Then in February, before the Olympics, I went to Australia, and I broke my collarbone! I couldn't believe it. I said to myself *"seriously?! What more can go wrong?"* but by this point, we had been through so much, everyone had had their individual setbacks, even though mine were often more unfortunate with the timings. I told myself, *"There wasn't any point worrying – what's worrying going to do? Absolutely nothing."* Get your head down, rehab and focus on what you can control. I can't spend my time thinking, *"what if I didn't fall over and break my collarbone? Why is this happening to me just before the Olympics?"* That sort of thinking would get me nowhere. Instead, I just focused on smashing rehab and taking the positive from the situation. I reframed the injury and said to myself *"you know what, I'm injured. I can't play hockey or even pick up a stick. However, I am going to get as fit as I possibly can be, so that when I return, I will be fitter than I would have been even without that injury."*

Ultimately, I think with setbacks, whether it's personal setbacks like catching meningitis or breaking my collarbone, or collective setbacks, like finishing eleventh in the World Cup or losing in the final of the Commonwealth Games, it's about focusing on what you can control and turning the negatives into positives. What some would see as adversity, others see as a challenge. I now just view adversities as problems that need to be solved and obstacles that need to be overcome, and that by doing so, it will make me better as a person. If everything was a smooth ride going into the Olympics, there's no way we would have won."

Team GB's Winning Habits

"When we are at tournaments, we always eat together. We also always wear the same kit. Our theory is that if a team is all wearing different bits of kit, they are not really together as a group. Another example is when we are out on the field, and the whistle is blown for half, or full time, we would always run in together, even when we were exhausted, it would show that we are together, alive and still have more to give. Other teams would all saunter into their changing rooms, and we would run past them. It really gets in other teams heads. On top of all this, we also have really challenging psychology sessions. We would get together as a group, and one by one stand up and say *"this is me on a good day, I am confident, or I am loud."* Or, *"this is me on a bad day, I am quiet, or I am reserved"*. You are encouraged to be open and tell everyone when you are not going through the best time or you are having a bad day. You would tell them about how you usually act on these sorts of days and how you would like to be spoken to by the rest of the team to get the best of their good spirits and to trigger anyone having a bad day to get back to a good day. Everyone would write it down. We did so many of these sessions that we knew each other so well. We would all know off and on the pitch whether the person is having a good day or a bad day."

How Lily Deals With Pressure On and Off The Pitch

"There are two types of pressure, external and internal. External pressure is pressure felt from things outside of yourself, like a boyfriend, parents, a huge crowd or coaches watching. Internal pressure is felt from inside of yourself, when you drive yourself crazy, telling yourself *"I want to play well in this game"* or *"I want to do well in this exam."* An activity I found useful to deal with this pressure was to write down three things I wanted to get out of what I was about to do. It would be three things I know I could control and deliver. For example, today I want to:

1. Look through these two lectures.
2. I want to write X amount of words.
3. I want to read X number of journals.

Then I don't drive myself crazy thinking what could I have done, or if I'm ready for this exam. It all comes back to one thing – focusing on what I can control."

The Importance Of 'Me Time'

"I also make sure that whatever I have got going on, that I make time for a bit of 'me time', where I can do whatever I want. I used to try and get everything done in my day; I now realise that everything is more productive when I give some time back to myself. During that 'me time' I can turn off, so when I go back and do something, I can do it better."

Whites and Coffee Don't Mix

"I was in the Olympic Village and where you get food is pretty much like a school canteen. There are all the groups with all the respective countries and sports sat together. It was a 'white day' for us, so I was in all white clothes. It was the day of our first game, and I was pretty nervous. I told myself *"get your breakfast, get it down you and then we will start preparing for the game ahead."* I got my coffee, my eggs and oats from the canteen. I had my entire tray loaded up; I also had a few glasses of water on there too to keep my hydration levels on point. I was just strolling back with my tray to the GB section of the canteen; walking past the French tennis section, with the likes of Gasquet nearby. I went to get the cutlery, holding the tray in one hand putting it off balance. Suddenly, the glasses of water tipped, and then the whole tray fell on me! A combination of coffee, eggs, oats and water all down my fresh whites. The plate then dropped off onto the floor and smashed. The French tennis team all turned around and were trying not to laugh. Everyone was looking, and I was just thinking to myself *"is it acceptable to crawl up into a ball right now?""*

15

Campaigners

"It always seems impossible until it's done."

–Nelson Mandela

"If you think you are too small to be effective, you have never been in bed with a mosquito."

–Bette Reese

Running A Charity For Young People With Cancer Alongside My Degree and Winning A £40,000 Prize For My Community Work
–HANNAH LARKIN

NAME: Hannah Larkin
UNIVERSITY: University of East Anglia
DEGREE: Biomedicine (BSc)

Hannah Larkin *(www.butterflygiving.co.uk)* is the student founder of Butterfly Giving, a charitable organisation which delivers bespoke 'Sunshine Boxes' to young people who have received a cancer diagnosis. Hannah also recently set up Butterfly Giving – Sunshine Families; a support group that connects families whose lives are affected by cancer. She won the Ambition AXA Award for her community work, which included a £40,000 prize and was presented with the Mayor's Award in recognition of her achievements.

The Butterfly Effect

"I met one of my now closest friends, George Soars, who had been diagnosed with Osteosarcoma at a very young age and was forced to have a leg amputated. I was a cadet with St. John's Ambulance at the time, and we were both assisting at a first aid competition at the National History Museum. I was looking after children who were innocently asking about what had happened to his leg. It was the first time I'd met him, but I gradually got to know George and was so inspired by his incredible attitude to life despite the challenges he'd faced. I decided to start raising money for various cancer charities. While they all do such fantastic work, nothing particularly reso-nated with exactly what I was hoping to achieve. I took a step back and began trying to connect directly with hospitals. The lightbulb moment came when I saw a quote which really struck a chord with me: "*It has been said that something as small as the flutter of a butterfly's wing can ultimately cause a typhoon halfway around the world*" – The Butterfly Effect. I knew that initially, I couldn't set up a charity to rival the likes of Cancer Research or Macmillan, but I could do everything in my power to make a few people's lives better while encouraging other people to do the same."

The Power Of 'NED'

"My best moments are always hearing that a young person who Butterfly Giving has helped is in remission. The acronym I've come to love is '*NED*' – No Evidence of Disease. Those are definitely the moments that I love the most."

The Story Of Jake

"The most pivotal moment for me was, unfortunately, losing a young lad who Butterfly Giving had worked with. Jake was one of the first recipients of a Sunshine Box and a complete inspiration. His will to keep fighting even when he was very ill made me realise just how privileged I am to be working with such amazing young people. Hearing that he'd passed away was the moment that impacted me the most as it really brought home the importance of what the charity was trying to achieve. Previously I'd wonder if the charity was actually making a difference – was it just a drop in the ocean compared to the many other much larger charities out there? This was until Jake's mum commented on a Butterfly Giving Facebook post, "*I can't thank you enough for what you did for my Jake*". That was really when everything started to become more real for me. I realised that Butterfly Giving was having a very tangible impact. We may not be funding cutting edge research, or raising millions of pounds. However, we are directly changing the lives of young people and their families and providing support when they need it most."

The Power Of Gratitude

"It's so easy to think that one bad mark in your course can be the end of the world but working with people my age and younger who have been diagnosed with cancer certainly puts these moments into perspective… While my problems may be legitimate, they become negligible when compared with what they're going through. These amazing young people sometimes go through more worries in one hospital appointment than I will likely ever experience during my time at university. One of the young ladies we worked with had to use a wheelchair after having a stroke due to chemotherapy. It was her simple wish to be able to re-learn the ability to move from a chair to a bed without a hoist or transfer board. It definitely makes me appreciate the small things. Above all, it fills me with gratitude knowing that I can play a small part in lives of such incredible young people."

To the student reading this who wants to set up their own charity, what would be your advice?

"My advice would be not to give up. Sometimes it can feel as if you're up against one hurdle after another, but however cliché this may sound, it's these moments that teach you invaluable lessons and help you to gain self-confidence in running a charity. Also, don't be afraid to get in touch with people who are already doing what you're doing. They may be ten times further on than you, but try to see every interaction as an opportunity for you to learn more and grow your own charity. Collaborate, make connections and don't be afraid to ask the 'silly' questions you think you should already know the answers to. Chances are, they're not silly, and you'll learn something new, and if they are, at least you've got some funny stories to look back on when you're successful!"

Co-Founding The Congolese Financial Project, Interning With Jeremy Corbyn and Being Shortlisted For TARGET jobs 'Undergraduate Of The Year'

−BENI NGWAMAH

NAME: Beni Ngwamah
UNIVERSITY: University of York
DEGREE: PPE (Philosophy, Politics and Economics) (BA)

Beni Ngwamah was born in the Democratic Republic of Congo, and his family migrated to the UK during his childhood to escape the outbreak of the civil war. Beni is one of the co-founders of COFIPRO (Congolese Financial Project), a fund designed to unite the Congolese diaspora and give its members access to low-interest loans. In his final year, he was selected as a representative of the UK in China in a program with Common Purposes and the Foreign & Commonwealth Office. He was also awarded the 'Highly Commended' award for outstanding contribution to student life with a Student-Led tutoring program that he co-founded and was shortlisted for TARGETjobs Undergraduate of the Year Award. Before arriving at university, Beni set up a football team to help create unity in his local community after three students at his school were stabbed to death, and in recognition of his achievements, Beni was invited to complete a two-week parliamentary placement with Labour Leader, Jeremy Corbyn.

How have your early life experiences in the Congo shaped your life?

"The Democratic Republic of Congo forms the bedrock of my ambitions. I was born in a time of upheaval and war with the Second Congo War named as the deadliest war in modern African history. In such a backdrop, I remember there was a call from the government to 'bring a machete, a spear, an arrow, to kill the Rwandan' which led to the formation of my earliest memory whereby the local people caught a rebel and burned him alive. Bearing witness to this amongst other things meant that I pretty much-reached adulthood at age seven. To make matters worse, our house was taken from us, and my mother flew to Europe in search of something better for us…. When people speak of poverty – I look back and think that was me. Having such a background has meant that I've always strived to make something of myself, to repay my mother for her sacrifice and to honour those who have a similar background to me in Congo."

'You Make Your Own Luck'

"Coming into uni, I tried everything and always consciously took myself out of my comfort zone because I knew that because of my background, my story of success will be far greater than of those who had a helping hand in life. It will resonate with younger generations and also possibly inspire them… I've always thought that I've never deserved anything in life so coming from nothing, eradicated any sense of entitlement or limitation. This meant that I approached life with the mindset that if it's possible, then I can do it. I remember reading about entrepreneurs, innovators and leaders and thinking there must have been a point in these people's lives where they stared down at failure and just went for it, and because of this thinking I'm always never afraid to fail. University's taught me that you do definitely make your own luck."

Appreciation As Motivation

"I always wondered what will be my legacy? When people will talk about me what will they say? If that didn't work, my mother would always motivate me. I'll think about the cleaning jobs she did, the hours she would spend breaking her back to put food on the table, the sacrifice she made leaving her children. That would usually help me in pushing through."

Beni On Staying Busy

"You actually have a lot more free time than you realise as a student. I always kept busy by filling up all the time I would ordinarily fill with Netflix, with activities and projects. I made sure it was the case that I could never say I was bored. Staying on top of everything was hard, but I downloaded handy planner apps and to-do lists. I would do my reading and exercises on the weekends, and in the weekday evenings, I would partake in the different projects I was involved in. There were times where I would be in the library at ungodly hours doing work but that's all part of the fun."

What's the best book you have ever read?

"My favourite book is *Heroes* by Robert Cormier. The book is set just after the end of the Second World War and is told in the first person by Francis Cassavant. The narrative moves between three time periods: what happened in Frenchtown as Francis was growing up, the events of the war, and the present. It's one of the best books for me because of its authenticity, how it captures the fragility of love and its exploration of other emotions. I read it at a moment in my life when I was transitioning from my teenage years. It made me aware of the world as it is."

Successfully Campaigning To Remove The 'Tampon Tax' From My University Campus

—IONA WAINWRIGHT

NAME: Iona Wainwright
UNIVERSITY: University of Exeter
DEGREE: Psychology and International Relations (BSc)

Iona Wainwright was one of the women's liberation officers (alongside Alisa Valpola-Walker, Meg Lawrence, Becky Howie and Eleanor Marsh) at the University of Exeter who successfully campaigned against the 'Tampon Tax'. Her campaign resulted in the University and Student Union Body covering the 5% cost of VAT from sales on tampons and sanitary towels at all shops on campus. The story was covered by The Huffington Post.

What is the 'Tampon Tax'?

"The tampon tax is a 5% luxury tax on menstrual products, such as sanitary towels and tampons. Menstruation is not a choice. It is not a luxury that someone decides to indulge in every month, so labelling menstrual products, as 'luxury items' is ridiculous. Anyone who menstruates requires these products and the tax adds to the financial burden of these necessary and essential products. This cost can be particularly difficult for low-income and homeless women."

Slogans + Petitions + Crocodile Steaks + Jaffa Cakes = Campaign Success

"We submitted a 'student idea' to our student council to sell menstrual products at a tax-free rate in our union shop. We ran a stall on International Women's Day, where we carried out a petition, collecting signatures from over 220 students and staff to put toward the national campaign. We also ran a photo petition, with signs such as *"The tampon tax is bloody ridiculous"* and *"Stop taxing periods. Period."* The response to this was amazing; so many people of all ages and genders were really supportive and got involved. We created a game in which we asked students to place items in one of two columns – items considered 'essential' by the government (such as crocodile steak, helicopters and Jaffa Cakes) and items considered 'luxury' and thus subject to the 5% tax. When people got involved, they were always really surprised to hear that tampons are considered luxury items, so we knew it was an important campaign as it raised a lot of awareness. We took these petitions to our student union as evidence of student support for the campaign, and we were able to get both the student union and the university to absorb the cost of the tax, so all outlets on campus now sell menstrual products at a tax-free rate."

Make People Identify With The Cause

"Find a way to connect the cause to students, so they identify with your message. There are so many campaigns being run at universities that it can be difficult for students to support them all. When they identify with the cause and can see clear, practical implications of the issue, we found that they were very willing to get behind the campaign. It is also really helpful to reach out to others who are involved in similar causes or campaigns."

What's the best book you have ever read?

"*A Thousand Splendid Suns* by Khaled Hosseini (who wrote *The Kite Runner*). It's about two women and their evolving friendship during great change and hardship in Afghanistan. The book tells a really touching story of sisterhood and female friendship."

Travelling Over 2,000 Miles With My Mates Across India In A Tuk Tuk And Raising $177,000 For Teenage Cancer Trust In The Process (With The Journey Getting Over 8.5 Million YouTube Views)

–MAX CANTELLOW

NAME: Max Cantellow
UNIVERSITY: University of Manchester (BSc)
University of Amsterdam (MA)
DEGREE: Business Management (BSc)

New Media and Digital Culture (MA) Max Cantellow *(IG: @maxc20, www.maxcantellow.com)* is a traveller, adventurer, photographer and blogger. Max travelled over 2,000 miles across India with seven close friends in three tuk-tuks. The four-part series entitled *The Rickshaw Run* was uploaded to *JacksGap* YouTube channel and currently has over 8,500,000 views in total. Max and his six friends raised $177,000 for Teenage Cancer Trust in the process. He has also embarked on a motorbike journey from New York City to Los Angeles, travelling through fourteen states and over 3,000 miles.

You Never Know What A Late Night Phone Call Can Lead To

"One night, my mate (Jack) called me and said, *"I know it's all a bit last minute, but what would you say if I suggested that we drove across India for a month?"* It was just one of those things that I couldn't say no to – and to the dismay of my parents – my answer was *"I'd say yes!"* I guess that's where all the madness began. Every second of the trip felt like you were on this crazy adventure with your best friends and you just never wanted it to end. So you embraced everything! Even the little things felt exciting, like building up our tuk-tuks with speakers and hooking up some power converters to batteries so we could charge our equipment. I felt like a kid again, as I was running around with heaps of energy and everyone else felt the same way; it was infectious!"

Travelling Gives Perspective

"Without sounding too cliché, travelling can give you some real perspective on the world that you are living in, but also into yourself as a person. You start to see how other people live in different cultures, and it can provide you with a real insight into your own life. You begin to compare what you have to other people in the world, which can make you feel extremely grateful and fortunate for the life you have and the position you are in. I always feel that every trip has changed me, even in the slightest of ways, it can be the way you look at something or the way you hold yourself or even just a slight change in your mannerism when handling a certain situation."

How To Travel On A Uni Student's Budget

"My number one tip would be to cook your own food. You can save lots of money doing this. There are so many students at university who are unable to cook themselves a decent meal and as a result, spend a fortune on eating out. Always have a few golden dishes up your sleeve. Doing this for a year could save you enough money to go travelling on! There are also so many ways of getting to another country on a budget, from car sharing to Couchsurfing. You just have to be creative and remember if there's a will, there's a way."

No Social Media Before Midday

"As I am pretty active online, it was very easy to just aimlessly scroll through things on my phone and to not engage with the present or what is in front of me. So I made some rules for myself, the big one that stuck was: no social media before midday… I began to realise that I would spend more time looking at what everyone else is up to in their lives in the morning, rather than concentrate on myself and what should be important to me. I started to become so much more productive by not opening up my Facebook messages or my notifications on Twitter or Instagram."

Creating Viral Student Union Campaigns Featured On BBC Radio 1, Buzzfeed, The Independent and The Huffington Post

—JASON MICHALSKI, BEN LEATHAM & TOBY GLADWIN

NAME: Jason Michalski
UNIVERSITY: Royal Holloway, University of London
DEGREE: Politics, Economics and International Relations (BSc)

Jason Michalski was elected Co-President of Sports and Development for the Students' Union of Royal Holloway (University of London) after his successful campaign video went viral. Within a week, his parody song received more than 70,000 views on YouTube and was covered by BBC Radio 1, The Independent and Buzzfeed.

NAME: Ben Leatham
UNIVERSITY: University of York
DEGREE: Philosophy (BA)

Ben Leatham became the student union president of the University of York after a successful campaign in which he saw his parody song played on BBC Radio 1 by DJ Scott Mills. Due to his successful presidency, Ben was nominated for the 'York Person Of The Year' award.

NAME: Toby Gladwin
UNIVERSITY: University of Exeter
DEGREE: Ancient History (BA)

Toby Gladwin became Guild President of the University of Exeter with the highest number of votes ever received by a candidate. His campaign video went viral and was covered by The Independent, Huffington Post and even a BBC Radio 1 interview.

How did the ideas for the most successful campaign videos come about?

Jason – "The campaign was all about building up the hype. We released a candidacy announcement video three days before the official start of the campaign week, and dropped screen shots and hints at a further, bigger video to come. That initial video got over a thousand views on YouTube in three days. When we finally released the Thrift Shop cover on YouTube, Facebook and Twitter, I had told my team to stagger the times at which they shared and liked it on social media so it would reach everyone slowly. However, I didn't realise that once the floodgates were opened, the video took on a life of its own. It became truly viral, and by the next day, I was on the phone with a local newspaper. By the third day it was featured on BBC Radio 1, and then it really took off and reached 50,000 views within seventy-two hours!"

Ben – "Having watched numerous videos from other Students' Union campaigns across the country, I knew I wanted to do something similar. My campaign team and I brainstormed a load of different ideas and decided on recording a music video inspired by *Let It Go* from the film *Frozen*. It was a massive operation. I had a group working on the lyrics, a group working on the filming and recording, and a load of extras. Within a day of releasing the video, it seemed like most people on campus had watched it or heard about it. The next thing we knew it was being played by Scott Mills on Radio 1. It was madness!"

Toby – "Basically the video was a combination of a lot of hard work from a few very talented friends. I will always be indebted to them but know they are proud of our creation! The 'viral' side of things kind of just happened. The first few days after the release was pretty quiet but then The Tab picked it up and spread it to other universities before Huffington Post wrote an article on it. It was a few weeks after I got elected that Radio 1 got in contact over Twitter and wanted to do an interview. That was an experience but, for me, the video had already done all I wanted it to, and the rest was just a bonus!"

What's the funniest moment from your time at university?

Jason – "Tennis club socials were always highlights. Clubs and societies would model for a Charity Naked Calendar during November. Naturally, we chose to take our picture on the outdoor tennis courts, which was chilly at that time of year. To get our clothes off we played "strip tennis", taking a piece of clothing off every time we lost a point."

Ben – "I would have to say the funniest moment of my time at university is equally the most bizarre. It came in my second year, on the day of Project D, a massive student event we had been organising for months. We had booked noughties chart topper Basshunter as the headline act, and when we were setting everything up in our college bar, he turned up and literally just strolled in through reception looking completely lost. It was just such a ridiculous situation."

Toby – "Me and my housemates played a game called Pub God, where the six of us each had a 'God Card' that meant at any time, day or night, we could play it, and all of us had to rush to the pub. Last one there bought the round, and this led to a lot of angst and exertion but a lot of fun."

Founding the UK's First University
Cancer Research Society (CRUKSOC)

–LUKE HART

NAME: Luke Hart
UNIVERSITY: University of Manchester
DEGREE: Physics (MPhys) Theoretical Cosmology (PhD)

Luke Hart has just finished the first year of his PhD in Theoretical Cosmology at the University of Manchester. From the second year of his undergraduate studies at the same university, he founded and chaired the Cancer Research UK Society (CRUKSOC). Balancing a schedule of captaining the American Football team, producing a show on university radio and participating in the musical theatre society, Luke guided the society to turn over just under £20,000 in charitable donations for Cancer Research UK during his tenure. The society is still running today, receiving the prestigious Fundraising Society of the Year Award and opened the floodgates for Cancer Research UK societies across the UK.

The Facebook Message That Changed Luke's Life

"I got a message on Facebook from an old, old friend who I had known for years but hadn't spoken to in a while. In that message, she told me she had Leukaemia. It was my first brush in my entire life with any type of cancer, and I was completely taken aback by the implications this was going to have on a close friend who was still at such a young age. Even though it was a friend and not a family member, which is the motivation for some people, it really cut me deep. I asked myself *"what can I do? Is there anything at all that I can do?"* If not for any particular reason than to do something positive about this, because it's a horrible, horrible thing that affects the lives of so many people."

How To Set Up Your Own Cancer Research Society

"Every SU will have records of what societies are active, so make sure you do the research for your particular university. I can't say enough about having a strong support group behind you, find people who are reliable because these sorts of ventures cannot be done alone. Find out who runs CRUK in your local area at a community level, see what events are coming up and see if there's anything you can do to help. If you want to set up your own events, just send an email to your local coordinator, Cancer Research will send you everything you need, from banners to posters to balloons. Our idea at CRUKSOC was to become the middleman between the charity and the students, and simply facilitate it so students don't have to organise anything, they just need to turn up and do a good deed."

The 3 Key Components To A Successful Charity Campaign

1. "Motivation – Surround yourself with people who are passionate, hardworking and will drive you further.

2. Prepare for difficulty – There'll be tough days where things don't go your way, you're all set up, and it's pouring with rain, and you get a small total, but you're doing something entirely voluntarily, so anything is a good thing!

3. Know when to say no! – Don't take everything on yourself, delegate to the competent people you've put around you so that you can actually enjoy your time at uni more."

What would be the one piece of advice you would give your younger self on your first day at university?

"Don't stress so much about your first year. I had a workaholic attitude in my first year. I lost out on forming stronger friendships because I was so focused on my work. Experience everything uni has to offer and balance your time! If you're not enjoying yourself, you're doing something wrong. Go out and get involved."

Providing Aid In Haiti, Increasing My Society's Sponsorship By 2000% and Meeting With The Executive Director of The UN Population Fund

—STEPHANIE IFAYEMI

NAME: Stephanie Ifayemi
UNIVERSITY: University of Warwick
DEGREE: Politics and International Studies (BA)

Stephanie Ifayemi flew out to Haiti to help with the relief effort after the 2010 earthquake that devastated so many lives. While in Haiti, Stephanie also worked with the Haitian Institute for Justice to help tackle the rape epidemic. She was the president of Warwick University's International Development Society; during her tenure, she turned the society around from the 'brink of ruin' and oversaw a 2000% increase in their sponsorship (from £890 to £20,000). The Warwick International Development Society Summit event hosted over 30 speakers such as Norman Finkelstein and Sir Richard Jolly, resulting in the event being regarded as one of the university's 'best ever conferences'. Stephanie's work has seen her meet with Secretary Justine Greening and the Executive Director of the UN Population Fund to discuss her activities. Stephanie was named fourth at the Rare Rising Stars UK's Top 10 Black Student awards, and also featured in Powerful Media's future leader's magazine. She is also part of the Young Leader UK (YLUK) network, a network for rising stars to foster and sustain strong relations between the US and the UK.

The Piece Of Wisdom From The Dalai Lama That Opened Stephanie's Eyes

"In his talk, the Dalai Lama said, "*The younger generation are our hope for the future – make an effort; [as] change comes through action*". I remember sitting in the audience feeling more and more driven, to not only continuously learn and engage, but that with hard work I too can one day make a difference – we all can. My trip to Haiti was the actualization of this – and it played a pinnacle role in my early steps and interests in International Development."

Stephanie's Emotional Journey In Haiti

"Being invited by prominent Haitian lawyer Mario Joseph and Brian Concannon, I worked with the Bureau des Avocats Internationaux (BAI) and the Institute for Justice and Democracy in Haiti (IJDH) to enforce Haitian human rights on two main projects: The Rape Accountability and Prevention Project (RAPP), as well as the Housing Rights and Advocacy project – mainly assisting in cases for trial. I additionally served as a liaison between Haitian attorneys and the Lawyers' Earthquake Response Network (LERN) of U.S. attorneys.

The RAPP Project was initiated to protect women and girls from the epidemic of rape in Haiti's Internally Displaced Persons (IDP) camps, and the Housing Rights Advocacy Project (HRAP), seeks to enforce the rights to housing in the IDP camps, especially the right against illegal eviction. Regarding my work on RAPP – the rape epidemic in Haiti was rife at this time, particularly for vulnerable women in camps for the displaced. Most memorable from my time in Haiti was a case that I worked on that went to trial just days before I left. It was the representation of an 11-year-old girl that had been raped by her father and subsequently bore his child. On the day of the trial, I remember sitting in the courtroom full of suspense as the judge gave her verdict. The man was sentenced to life imprisonment, and I could never forget the emotion and cries that bestowed the room that day. I felt overjoyed that we had won the case but also a deep sense of emotion – knowing this was one case out of many. I met a number of other girls between the ages of 11-16 that faced similar circumstances, but not all had received the same justice."

How To Throw A Popular Conference

"Honestly, don't be put off by the number of rejections you may get – as I remember the first few months were tough for us and our speaker list wasn't getting very far. So we rethought our strategy and continuously re-adapted our approach to suit different speakers; results will come if you persevere. I truly learnt the importance of using a quick initiative when it comes to hosting an event; always think of possible ways to harness and merge the skills of your team. Put yourself out there, and truly 'sell your vision' to the people around you, and wherever you go. Empathy is truly important, and thinking – *"what are the students attending this event looking for? How do we engage with busy, high-profile speakers and convince them that our event is worth attending?"* These were questions that we first addressed and tackled."

How Stephanie Stays Motivated

"What motivates me in difficult situations is remembering what drives me and why I want to succeed. I am inspired by a few greats from the past and what they managed to achieve in their lifetime. I printed off some quotes from leaders such as Martin Luther King and stuck them around my room as motivational triggers. This was particularly useful when it came to the weeks before final exams. Equally, I would again say identifying your working patterns is really important. I try to know when I need to take a break, to visit a friend, or just go out to eat or order a takeaway. I tend to work better when I'm happy, so I use this time out to refresh my mind, then go straight back to work after with a clearer perspective."

Stephanie's Clicking Habit

"I recently started beginning my day by clicking my fingers. A click for every second. It is quite daunting that with every click, is time that we will never get back. I use this as a reminder to try and utilise my day as best possible."

Setting Up A Student Mental Health Awareness Campaign Which Ended Up On BBC News

–GEORGE WATKINS

NAME: George Watkins
UNIVERSITY: Cardiff University
DEGREE: English Literature and Philosophy (BA)

George Watkins is a student mental health campaigner. Just seven weeks into his first term at uni, George set up 'The Mental Youth' – a campaign to help all students suffering from any form of mental health issue. His work has led him to be interviewed by the BBC multiple times for TV and radio, which saw him open up about his struggles with his own personal mental health problems, as well as his opinions on the current state of mental health treatments in the UK. George is currently performing a UK-wide mental health survey of university students and is in the process of collating his work into a book.

How do you personally define mental health?

"Mental health, at a fundamental level, is the same as physical health. There is a definite connection between body and mind that works like a balancing scale. If there is excessive stress placed on the mind, much like an injury to the body, it can begin to struggle to bear the weight. Anxiety and depression are both common feelings, but the conditions themselves refer to very physical conditions. Psychosomatic research has proved that depression has some very physical symptoms, as does anxiety, that persist in a circular pattern over time. Usually, it follows a course of *Stressor- Mental Response- Physical Response- Stressor,* with the mental response often being thoughts like *"I can't cope"* and *"It's all too much to bear"*, and the physical responses being insomnia or panic attacks. This works in a cycle, as the mind and body become exhausted as the cycle repeats itself, and the stressor's weight is felt much more heavily each time."

Why do you think university students are vulnerable to mental health issues?

"For any student, there are pressures of exam stress, growing up and trying to find a sense of identity, but I think for university students it is much greater. I believe that it's largely down to a sudden feeling of isolation and detachment from the comfort and security of childhood and family ties, usually living alone and dealing with adult issues that are often previously approached, such as drugs, jobs and sex. There is a distinct lack of availability of counselling services, thanks to both the government persistently shredding youth mental health budgets, but also thanks to a lack of conversation among students as a whole about something that really should be mentioned as much as sexual health or physical health."

The Power Of A Dog And Creative Outlets

"I hid away and distracted myself from my mental health problems, hoping that by not giving them attention, they would vanish – which they didn't. As time passed, I began to open up to myself about what I was suffering with…When I was trapped in my house for so long by agoraphobia, my only source of company for most days was my dog, and I think his sense of companionship really helped me get through some really dark days. In many ways, he acted as a disability dog. Music and writing were my creative outlets – and they still are! The best way I have found to manage my issues was to talk to people and to be honest and frank about why I might seem to act strange sometimes."

Fix The Problem, Not The Symptoms

"Cognitive Behavioural Therapy as a form of counselling that can work wonders, as it particularly emphasises the elimination of negative thinking to try and tackle the cycle I mentioned earlier. Other holistic methods could help, but unless you deal with the underlying problems, the mental health issue is unlikely to be solved. Giving someone paracetamol for a broken arm might help relieve the pain for a while, but it won't actually fix the problem."

If someone reading this suspects that they may be suffering from a mental health condition or suspects a friend may be – what would be your advice to them?

"Talk. Talk to your friends. Talk to your family. Go and see your GP and see what forms of counselling they can offer. Speak to your counselling services on campus. Remember that you aren't alone. 1 in 4 people will have a mental health problem at some point in their life, which equates to nearly 2 billion people worldwide. If you suspect a friend may be suffering from a mental health condition, my advice would again be to talk to them. Try to understand what's going on, and encourage them to speak to a professional, such as their university counselling services or their GP. Being there for them can be invaluable."

Interviewing David Cameron And Nick Clegg on BBC1 And Regularly Running Marathons For Autism Awareness

—PETER GILLIBRAND

NAME: Peter Gillibrand
UNIVERSITY: University of Exeter
DEGREE: Philosophy, Politics and Economics (PPE) (BA)

Peter Gillibrand is a student political and charity campaigner. He is a contributor for BBC Generation, has appeared on programmes on BBC Radio 1 and Radio 4 and has interviewed then Prime Minister David Cameron and Deputy Prime Minister Nick Clegg on BBC 1. Peter regularly engages in charity work, frequently running marathons for Autism awareness as well as being co-president for his university's RAG committee. When he is away from university, Peter spends his time leading 'Summer Adventures', a project that takes seventy carers and provides them with a well-needed rest from their difficult responsibilities.

'Opportunities Are Everywhere'

"I was selected from a group of two hundred to be one of ten people who got the chance to interview David Cameron on BBC Radio 1. On another occasion, when he was campaigning on the EU Referendum, he came to talk to the students at my uni. I managed to get on television by challenging him on the Welsh Steel crisis, which got national coverage and posed a really serious question. The opportunities are everywhere, just be active in finding them while at university!"

Peter's Motivation Behind His Charity Work

"My motivation behind this is my severely autistic brother, Adam. He was diagnosed before I was born and is in full-time care. I just want to be able to give back to carers by raising money to ensure that they have all the help that they can get. I have recently finished a project leading a summer camp for young carers that helped me to give back to these amazing people. This passion for giving back has also influenced my interest in running, and so far, I have done two full marathons and a further ten half-marathons, raising lots of money for charities in the process. In the future, I hope to raise even more by doing the Marathon Des Sables as well as the Antarctica marathon! If you can, I would really recommend getting into your RAG society, as not only is it good for your CV, but you're able to do so much more than you'd think (at uni) and gain so many skills, all while raising money for amazing people who deserve it."

What's the funniest moment of your time at university?

"I would have to say having to go to Alcoholics Anonymous after a rugby social is definitely a favourite. Unfortunately, I got a bit too drunk after the social and ended up being banned from Exeter City Centre for a day! It was all in good spirit and nothing that bad, just a funny situation from a way too drunk fresher at a heavy social. I'd also have to say that sitting with a homeless lady with a guitar singing *Wonderwall* after a social was one of the highlights – all of us gave a total of around £150 to her too – she was a great singer!"

Beating Cancer For The Third Time
(In My Fresher Year At University!)

–CHANDOS GREEN

NAME: Chandos Green
UNIVERSITY: Chichester University
DEGREE: Social Work (BA)

Chandos Green is a student social campaigner who has defied all odds by beating a brain tumour not once, not twice, but three times. His amazing story went viral online, which resulted in his story being featured on ITV News and he now regularly raises money for young people with cancer.

Chandos' Incredible Story

"I was diagnosed at the age of three with a benign (non-cancerous) tumour towards the middle of my brain after experiencing difficulties with movement down my left-hand side. I then had my first surgery and had to have MRI scans every few months post-op. At the age of six, the residual tumour began to grow back, so I need a second operation. Unfortunately, I ended up in intensive care with a bleed and swelling on the brain. Three days later – the surgery was re-attempted. This surgery went well, but still, part of the tumour remained. In my second term at university, I started having headaches and memory problems. It was after a few small blackouts and occasions where I was losing my balance that I went in for an MRI scan. It was the day after my nineteenth birthday when I received the diagnosis that I had my third tumour. Two months later I went in for another operation."

Live Each Day One At A Time

"I have seen how overnight your life can change because of illness and I don't take things for granted. In the past two years, I have kind of developed the perspective that I cannot change my circumstances, nor would I want to do so because it has enabled me to see the beauty in everyday life, and I now enjoy living every day at a time."

'Just Do You'

"There have been a lot of times where I couldn't cope, and I have had to call my mum or best friends for help. But I think it's important now to take it step by step. The worst thing you can do is rush something… The advice I'd give to students is the same advice my friend gave me after my last operation *"just do you"*. It can be easy to follow the crowd and not be yourself because you are worried about what other people think of you, but university enables you to meet so many new people (so try and find people where you can be yourself)."

Entrepreneurs

""I think it's very important to have a feedback loop. I think that's the single best piece of advice: constantly think about how you could be doing things better and questioning yourself."

– Elon Musk

"An entrepreneur is someone who will jump off a cliff and assemble an airplane on the way down."

– Reid Hoffman

Setting Up A Property Empire In The Final Year Of My Degree (Now Worth Over £4,000,000 And Winning 'Deal Of The Year' At The Property Investment Awards)

—ALEX SZEPIETOWSKI

NAME: Alex Szepietowski
UNIVERSITY: University of York
DEGREE: PPE (Philosophy, Politics and Economics) (BA)

Alex Szepietowski *(www.alexszepietowski.com)* is a property investor and entrepreneur. In his final year of university, Alex set up two property businesses despite having no expertise and living on a student budget. His portfolio has subsequently grown, and he now owns over £4,000,000 worth of property, which consists of twenty-six houses and flats. Alex has given a TEDx talk that has over 1,000,000 YouTube views, won an Institute of Directors Director of the Year Award, and won Deal of the Year at the Property Investment Awards.

The Power Of A Mentor

"If you find a mentor whose values you align with and who has achieved what you want – it's the best investment you can ever make."

Did you ever have any problems in getting people to take you seriously due to your age?

"Age is only a 'thing' if you make it one. At first, my limiting beliefs were a lack of money, a lack of knowledge and a lack of experience. All these beliefs were valid, but we can all find 'valid' excuses to play small or give up on chasing a life we want. As soon as my mindset shifted, I realised I was in control of what I could achieve and that I could learn and refine a simple, replicable and incredibly powerful business model by providing a win-win-win for my investors, tenants and myself. At this point, doors started flying open."

'Where Time Goes, Energy Flows And Results Show'

"I chose modules at university based on what I knew I could get good grades in, which was mainly essays. I locked myself away for two weeks and bashed out a good essay. Exams were tougher as you had to learn the whole syllabus, so I shied away from those where I could, or I set up study groups where we all did a bit of reading and compiled the notes together to save time. (As Alex was the head of the study group, it meant that he didn't even have to take notes!)…I would be lying if I said I smashed partying, socialising, business and my degree. I chose to prioritise my business in my final year as I'd done a lot of partying in the previous years. There's no right or wrong, but each choice produces a different result. As they say *"where time goes, energy flows and results show."* I now have more time for all the other things – but also I am a more balanced person and see the importance of making sure all areas of my life are being addressed at any one time."

What's the best book you have ever read?

"*Rich Dad Poor Dad* by Robert Kiyosaki – a must read for anyone reading this who hasn't read it already. I knew that I didn't want to have to work forever for a pay cheque. I decided there were far simpler and quicker ways to become financially self-sufficient than working sixty-hour weeks for someone else, just to get paid and save up deposits for houses!"

Setting Up A Marketing Agency In The First Year Of My Degree That Raised £100,000 Via Crowdfunding In 24 Hours (And Has Represented Ronaldinho!)

−BENJAMIN JEFFRIES

NAME: Benjamin Jeffries
UNIVERSITY: University of Bath
DEGREE: Business Administration (BSc)

Ben Jeffries *(IG: benwjeffries)* is an entrepreneur and founder of Influencer. *(FB/IG: @InfluencerCo, www.influencer.uk)*, which is a marketing agency that connects global brands with people that have a large following on social media platforms. Despite being a young company, Influencer has already worked with stars such as Ronaldinho and Joanna Kuchta as well as large brands that include Happn, Uber, Crowdmobile and Daniel Wellington. Influencer has a combined reach of over 300,000,000 potential consumers, was shortlisted for the Virgin Media StartUp Awards and raised £100,000 in just twenty-four hours via crowdfunding website Crowdcube.

How Ben Came Up With The Idea For Influencer

"I had a small clothing business called Breeze, and I used to try and get in touch with people who had large social media followings to see if they would wear the products. I found that the majority of these 'celebrities' would either ignore you or charge ridiculous amounts, while their marketing agencies would say that I needed a minimum of £15,000 to spend, which is unfeasible for a young start-up. This gave me the light bulb moment that led to Influencer. An agency that allowed small companies to work on any budget size and make it easy for start-ups to boost their business right from the beginning."

Ben On Taking Risks

"I'm extremely driven and have always liked to have a project along-side my studies, so it wasn't really an issue with regards to pushing myself to 'go do it'. At the end of the day – we're young, we don't have to support a family, so we can take much bigger risks."

Write A Business Plan

"A business plan is a lot of effort but honestly worth doing. Simply because it helps you have a clear vision of the future of the business and keeps you on the right track. Of course, as a start-up, your business plan will likely change almost every week – but it's a good guide to have along the way."

Is it a disadvantage to be young in business?

"Completely mixed – sometimes it's an advantage and sometimes it a disadvantage. As I mentioned earlier, it's an advantage as you're able to take much bigger risks – if it fails; it's not the end of the world. Did you know James Dyson created 5,126 failed prototypes of his vacuum before finally succeeding? However, there are some disadvantages to being young and part of the 'millennial' generation. Last year, I'd arranged for a meeting with a prospective client at their offices, and upon arriving (looking my twenty-year-old self), their attitude towards me was completely different from how they'd been acting over the phone and via email. They started to patronise me, calling my company an *"awesome little project that just wasn't the right size for them."* That was genuinely one of the lowest points since setting up the company."

The Importance Of Planning and Keeping Up Social Appearances

"It's all about self-control otherwise you can end up staying up 'till 3 AM replying to emails. Maintaining a healthy balance is important, or it will all just get too much. I like to ensure that I have planned the day ahead; that could be working from 8 AM until 12 PM, then hitting the gym for a couple of hours and returning to work until 7 PM. It's important to keep up social appearances, or you may drive yourself crazy."

Act Now

"The most important piece of advice I could give relates to a favourite quote of mine – *"The best time to plant a tree was 20 years ago. The second best time is now."* If you think you have the next 'billion dollar idea' then go out and make it happen. Don't ever use the excuse *"but I've got no money to execute it"* – think innovatively on how to reach out to people who do have the money; whether that be sending out a tweet or handwriting them a letter."

Co-Founding An International Music Platform For University Students And Being Named 'Student Entrepreneur To Watch' By The Huffington Post

–NICK HAMPSON

NAME: Nick Hampson
UNIVERSITY: University of Oxford
DEGREE: Music (BA)

Nick Hampson is the co-founder of the music platform 'Vulture Sessions'. The platform was set up with his co-founder Jack Saville as a way of providing instant high-quality music content on a regular basis. They filmed, edited and published videos as well as organised concerts. Vulture Sessions helped people watch 'amazing high-quality content from universities all over the world and enabled young artists to get their work seen by a large audience'. The platform expanded in the UK to Reading, Oxford, Manchester and London as well as in the USA, to Miami, Indiana, Virginia and Harvard. The Huffington Post named Nick 'The Student Entrepreneur to Watch' after starting Elixa, a social payment aggregation app for funding group experiences. Nick's band has headlined shows in London and Reading, and Nick has done two solo shows in New York. He recently co-directed and produced his first film, *Wilders*, a documentary on controversial Dutch politician Geert Wilders.

How Nick Used The 'Facebook Model'

"The logic is that 'if something works at one major university, it has a damn good chance of working at all of them', much like Facebook's initial marketing method. We knew there would be similar numbers of talented musicians at other universities around the world and turned our focus to setting up Vulture teams on other campuses – something I learned very quickly was a tremendously difficult thing to do. Over time we launched eight other locations, all putting out content through one streamlined channel. We had somehow created a recognisable brand without necessarily intending to."

Work Harder Than The Next Guy

"After launching in all these new places, we found ourselves sitting in the offices at Universal Music and Island Records every few weeks telling them about great unsigned artists that we'd found around the world. This all happened over about a year and a half, proving to me that the key catalyst to entrepreneurial success is working harder than the next guy."

Have you ever had any problems with getting people to take you seriously due to your age?

"I believe how seriously people take you in business is much more about backing yourself and confidence than age or experience. This comes from having a deep connection with your vision and product. If you really believe you're building something awesome, so will everyone else."

What would be the one piece of advice you would give your younger self on your first day at university?

"Don't waste a single hour. University is one of the best times in your life where everything is possible, and it goes by faster than you can imagine. I'm sitting writing this in New York, where I now work having graduated two months ago and have to remind myself that I'm not going back in October for another year. It's a tiny window of time where there is a support system that allows you to achieve just about anything you want if you work hard enough. That's a very special thing."

What is the best book you have ever read?

"I really like *Anthem* by Ayn Rand. It's about a world where the concept of 'I' or 'the self' does not exist. Everyone refers to themselves as we and others as they. The entire concept of identity is completely subverted. I found it to be one of the most meaningful portrayals of society that I'd ever read. Ultimately, the main character discovers the concept of the self. Quite an amazing journey and a good example of a book which creates a dystopian world which is scarily familiar."

What's the funniest moment of your time at university?

"I managed to convince my friend Rosie to become vegetarian. However, on the second day of her vegetarianism, we had been out drinking and stopped at a kebab van on the way home. While I'm ordering, Rosie starts screaming behind me, having accidentally put a friend's chicken strip in her mouth and chewed. I'll never forget the image of her frantically running off to a side street in a panic to spit it out in private, having only been vegetarian for about twenty-four hours!"

Founding Depop's Best Selling Handmade Lingerie Clothing Line

–CHELSEA PEARL LI

NAME: Chelsea Pearl Li
UNIVERSITY: SOAS – University of London
DEGREE: International Management (China) (BSc)

Chelsea Pearl Li *(IG: @lilipearluk, www.lilipearl.myshopify.com)* is an entrepreneur, fashion designer, model, actress and social media personality. Chelsea is the founder of LiLiPEARL, which is a handmade lingerie and clothing line. LiLiPEARL was the number one seller on Depop, a peer-to-peer social shopping app with over three million users worldwide. She has previously been cast in *James Bond Skyfall*, *The Inbetweeners 2*, *Muppets Most Wanted*, *Ex Machina* and reality TV show *Made in Chelsea*.

How Chelsea Went From Sketching Designs In Her Spare Time To Launching A Number One Best Seller

"In my spare time, I'd find myself sketching designs or lusting over beautiful and expensive pieces of clothing. During university, I was also a huge party girl, so was always looking for great outfits to wear. After wearing my own stuff out, I was noticing a lot of girls asking where I got my outfits from (either through Facebook, Instagram or in person, and also asking if I can make them stuff), so I just thought why not just start my own line? I started LiLiPEARL as a hobby, just selling a few statement pieces here and there on eBay for a bit of extra pocket money. I then joined Depop, and it went crazy from there. After a few months, I'd become their top-seller worldwide, even though I was still selling and dispatching items from my bedroom. Since then, it's been non-stop photo shoots and interviews, and as I was coming up to the end of my degree, I realised that this is what I really loved doing and I may as well just go for it."

Chelsea's Idea Notebook

"I'm always carrying a little notebook with me so that I can jot down any ideas whenever I have them. And as soon as I get an idea, I'll want to crack on with it as soon as I can."

Turning Customers Into Models

"I think LiLiPEARL has managed to develop a large fan base by actually creating it organically. A lot of the photos on our social media are real customer photos as opposed to generic catalogue images. Girls come in all shapes and sizes, and with shopping online, it can be hard to see what some things will look like on as the majority of companies use super skinny or tall girls to model their clothes, which can often be an unrealistic comparison for most girls. For me personally, it's an issue as I'm pretty short! By tagging and featuring customers wearing our stuff, we've created a sort of interactive Instagram account whereby potential customers are able to see our LiLiPEARL items on real girls and compare this to how the items would look on them. And for the customers that have already bought from us, it's always a compliment to be featured and shown off via social media!"

You Are The Average Of The People You Hang Around With

"To be successful, in any field, one must surround themselves with like-minded, supportive and positive people. One of my biggest mistakes was allowing negative and unsupportive people into my life who constantly made me feel drained and not good enough to be successful."

Chelsea's Google Throwback Motivation Technique

"Everybody has to start somewhere. One of my favourite ways of motivating myself is googling what people did before they were successful. For example, did you know Kanye West worked for GAP when he was younger? It really makes you realise that if you keep working hard – anything is possible."

What's the best book you have ever read?

"My favourite books are the *Freakonomics* books by Steven Levitt and Stephen Dubner. I love what they did with applying economic theory to the real world, and its darker areas. Though rather controversial, it's a fascinating read."

What's the funniest moment from your time at university?

"One day in my third year, one of my tutors wanted me to see her to discuss one of my final essays. I dreaded the meeting because I thought she'd have a go at me for always being late or missing lectures. Somehow we ended up going off topic and talking about my business. In the end, she was checking out my clothing website and even invited me to do a talk for the entrepreneur's society at my university. It was kind of awkward showing her my lingerie line though, especially as I model a few items!"

Starring In A Barclays Advert, Consulting Tesco And Calvin Klein And Donating £40,000 Of The Profits Made To UNICEF

−SOHAIL IQBAL

NAME: Sohail Iqbal
UNIVERSITY: Aberystwyth University
DEGREE: Biology (BSc)

Sohail Iqbal is a student who founded a consultancy business that has worked with companies such as RBS, Tesco, Calvin Klein, The Foreign Office and NRDC Equity Partners. He has donated over £40,000 of his earnings (while he was a student) to UNICEF and is an ambassador to the Walk Free Charity and Children of Peace. Sohail's work was recognised by UNICEF and the UN and was given a personal tour of their buildings in New York. He was also featured in a Barclays advert in his time at university.

If You Produce Results, They Won't Care How Old You Are

"Sure I was at university, but when these brands want to lure in younger demographics, I managed to talk a lot of them into changing their mind or becoming comfortable with the idea (of being consulted by a young person). To ease their mind, I offered them incentives. So a week trial, a reduced rate or even some free overtime work. But it all came down to the bottom line; I did what was expected on time and within budgets set out. Once you've done that for one project, they'll come back with ten more asking for your involvement and creativity."

Time Management Advice From A Student Who Balanced His Degree With Consulting Tesco And Calvin Klein

"The one thing that helped me manage my time was a list. All I needed was a pen and paper. Jot down what needs to be done and cross them out one by one. (If you want to make your lists digital – download Wunderlist – it enables you to access your to-do lists on your phone and your laptop. You can also set push notification reminders and expected completion dates.)"

What Motivated Sohail To Give £40,000 Of His Earnings To UNICEF

"I've been keeping an eye on Syria since the start of the civil war. I think the moment that really made me think was when I was speaking to a Holocaust survivor, and she said how much the whole Syrian crisis reminded her of herself when she was a child fleeing Nazi Germany. I had already seen some pretty bad pictures from Syria, I was in contact with people too, but that really made me think. As humans, we are supposed to learn from our mistakes. Clearly, we still have a lot of learning to do. So in a nutshell, I decided that I would donate my income to charity as I thought it would be much better than sitting in an account somewhere. I also told my clients who were over the moon and eventually they decided to pay or donate more. It was a win-win situation; I was given more work and exposure while helping some of the most vulnerable children in the world. Thanks to the donations I was even given a tour of the UN and UNICEF buildings when I went to New York last year."

What would be the one piece of advice you would give your younger self on your first day at university?

"I would tell myself *"Enjoy it. It's going to be amazing"*. Now that I've left university I can honestly say it was the best three years of my life. If I could go back I would change so much; I would stop the stupid fights with friends, the drama and just enjoy it. Go out more, have fun and study a bit harder."

What's the best book you have ever read?

"*The Grand Design* by Stephen Hawking. The book really made me think. It's also unlike other physics books in that it doesn't have a lot of maths and scientific mumbo jumbo in it. When it comes to books, I always stick to ones that can actually make me think about the world around us, so this ticked that box perfectly."

What's the funniest moment from your time at university?

"I have many, and almost all of them involve alcohol! But the funniest moment has to be having my friend, Hannah, pierce my ear during pre-drinks in the communal kitchen. I don't even think we sterilised the needle properly. The result? My left ear was pierced, and I wore a love heart earring for three odd weeks."

The UK's Best Up And Coming Student Entrepreneurs (The Winners Of The Shell LIVEwire Smarter Future Award, The Hyundai Skills For The Future and Prince Andrew's Young Entrepreneur Award)

—RAVI TOOR, CALLUM COLES AND PHIL DANESHYAR

NAME: Ravi Toor
UNIVERSITY: University of Leeds
DEGREE: Environment and Business (BA)

Ravi Toor is the CEO and Founder of Filamentive – a sustainable 3D printing material brand, turning waste plastic into usable 3D Printing filament. Ravi won the Shell LIVEwire Smarter Future award, which is an award for the best young start-up providing solutions to the UK's sustainability challenges. In the process, he was also short-listed for Young Entrepreneur of the Year.

NAME: Callum Coles
UNIVERSITY: University of Bath
DEGREE: Computer Science (BSc)

Callum Coles is a student entrepreneur who founded SoberDrive. SoberDrive designed physical preventatives to drink driving, includ-ing a breathalyser within a car key that uses the result of a breath test to determine whether or not the car's ignition can be started. Callum's entrepreneurial spirit was featured on BBC Breakfast, and he was the winner of Hyundai Skills For the future award.

NAME: Phil Daneshyar
UNIVERSITY: University of York
DEGREE: PPE (Politics, Philosophy and Economics) (BA)

Phil Daneshyar is the founder of the technology start-up Thirsti. Thirsti's product, the puck, is placed into a water bottle and tracks how much the customer has drunk, determines when the customer is dehydrated and needs to drink and reminds them with in-app notifications. Phil received over £140,000 of investment for his idea and won the Duke of York's Young Entrepreneur award.

Is age ever an issue?

Ravi – "I mention that I founded the business while at university but generally I let the products, company culture and (hopefully) my salesmanship do the talking. When we get to the face-to-face meetings stage, they may realise my age, but by that point, they already like the product or company. My tip would be to look as big of a company as you can, without being too misleading."

Phil – "You can become experienced by 'experiencing' – so just do it. Those who mistreat you and dismiss you as naïve will seem foolish once they walk into a store to buy your product."

Always Be Critical Of Your Idea

Callum – "If you're just starting out with an idea, be critical of it yourself; it is very easy to pretend an idea has no faults when it's your own. If you have properly evaluated your idea, you will already be aware of the faults and can work on a solution.

Although it can be hard to critique your own idea, it will be hugely beneficial if, when discussing the idea, you can show you have thought about every aspect of it."

You've Got Nothing To Lose At University

Phil – "My mindset was always; if I fail, it doesn't matter because I'll get my degree, get a job and it will be like it never happened. You've nothing to lose at this age, especially at university."

Switch Between Tasks

Callum – "I find my most successful way of maintaining a constant work ethic is by switching tasks and never working on one particular task for more than two hours unless absolutely necessary. I find switching in this way between university work and business allows me to keep my concentration, so there really is meaning to the expression that change is as good as a rest."

What is the best book you have ever read?

Ravi – "*The Chimp Paradox* by Steve Peters. It has, without a doubt, helped me self-reflect, make changes to my life and improve as an individual."

Callum – "*Tricks of the Mind* by Derren Brown. Amongst the magical trickery of the book, there is a great deal of psychology that I found particularly interesting. Reading this book is probably one of the reasons I do not take my age as a disadvantage, as all ages are susceptible to suggestion and influence."

Phil – "*The Alchemist* by Paulo Coelho. It's a story with a strong theme of the continuous pursuit of happiness. I had read it before I started my business and it reminds me of Steve Job's famous talk at Stanford where he says *"you can only connect the dots looking backwards"*. The book reminds you that even if things in life aren't going so well right now, they will in the end, and that where you get to is the result of everything you've done."

Founding The UK's Number One Student Money Website
—OWEN BUREK

NAME: Owen Burek
UNIVERSITY: University of Manchester
DEGREE: Geography (BA)

Owen Burek is the CEO of Save the Student! *(FB: @savethestudent, www.savethestudent.org)*, the leading student money website in the UK with over two million visits per month. He started Save the Student! in his first year at university and it has since grown into a viral social enterprise. Every week they send out a weekly newsletter to thousands of students highlighting the best student deals and discounts. Owen has also written for The Guardian, The Independent, and has appeared on BBC News.

Success Can Often Just Be A Numbers Game

"Save the Student! was just one of the maybe one hundred to one hundred and fifty websites that I started, but it was the only one that really took off. I had so many random sites running, I even had one for mobility scooters! I guess Save the Student took off because I was able to write about the topic as a student myself, so it was easier to write interesting content."

Owen's Three Tips To Save Money At University

1. "Students get a big lump sum appearing in their bank account when their student loan drops, and it's easy to go on a night out and spend a bit more than you'd have liked to, just because the money is there. Drip feed money from a savings account to your

current account, it makes it a lot harder to blow all your cash. Try to find a high-interest savings account that allows you to withdraw money at any point, and transfer money every month into the current account that you spend out of.

2. Utilise student discounts! Ask for freebies and money off every single time. Retailers don't always advertise discounts and students don't usually ask, whether it's out of awkwardness or just forgetting. At worst, they'll just say no."

3. Take advantage of bank switching. In August the big banks tend to release their offers to entice new students into opening accounts with them. You can get all sorts, some banks have offered four year 16-25 Railcards, larger 0% overdrafts or higher interest paid on balances. Shop around every year and switch your bank to get the best deal."

What are some uncommon tips for making money that the average student isn't aware of?

1. "Matched betting – It's an increasingly popular way for students to make money without any risk. Check out our guide on *www. savethestudent.org/make-money/what-is-matched-betting*.

2. Task-based Work – Conventional jobs aren't always the best option for students. Freelancing and doing work online is much more flexible to fit around studies and other commitments. Task based work, providing you have the skills to do it, can give you better pay without being tied into a contract. I did a load of graphic design work at uni, and that also gave me great experience for my job today! Try *peopleperhour.com* or *upwork.com*."

The Best Time To Take Risks

"Every student should start a business. I'm not talking on a national scale or disrupting an entire industry. It can be done on a really small scale – like selling items on Amazon. It'll give you so much more confidence and experience than a regular student job. A friend of mine started a club night when he was at university, and he's now made a career out of it, so you have no idea where it may lead. Even if it doesn't work out, you'll have something you've started off your own back that will really impress employers or give you lessons to take forward to future ventures. As a student, you don't have many responsibilities, so this is the best time to take these sorts of risks!"

What would be the one piece of advice you would give your younger self on your first day at university?

"Stick with it! Save the Student didn't take off for nearly three years. I love the excitement of starting a new project, creating the logos and the designs, so it would have been easy to stop it and start something else. I didn't do anything with it at all for nearly a year, it was just sat online with no new content, but it started picking up traffic as the articles that were on there filled the gaps in the Google search results. After a while, I started getting contacted by advertisers who wanted to advertise on the site, and that's when I realised it was a real business I could grow to support me long term."

What's the funniest moment from your time at university?

"Our house caused a lot of hilarious moments. It was a joke. The kitchen ceiling fell through and nearly hit my housemate, and we had a toilet that kept leaking through the floorboards over the front door entrance. It wasn't always funny at the time, but it's funny now looking back at it."

Founding A Worldwide Shop For Unique Jewellery, Receiving Blogging Awards From InStyle Magazine and Cosmopolitan And Interviewing Bradley Cooper and George Clooney

—EM SHELDON

NAME: Em Sheldon
UNIVERSITY: Leeds University
DEGREE: Broadcast Journalism (BA)

Em Sheldon *(IG/TW: @emshelx, www.emtalks.co.uk)* is a blogger, entrepreneur, online influencer and social media personality. Em is the writer behind the beauty, fashion, travel and lifestyle blog EmTalks. The blog has over 5 million views and received various awards including InStyle Magazine's Top Lifestyle and Travel Blogger and Cosmopolitan Newcomer Award. Since setting up EmTalks, she has been featured on Capital FM, BBC Radio, Cosmopolitan Magazine, InStyle Magazine and has worked with global brands such as Adidas, Asos and Clinique. She is also the founder of LVNDR, an online shop for costume jewellery designs at affordable prices that won the Sir Peter Thompson award for enterprise. The multi-talented Em is also a broadcast journalist who has reported at the Olympics and the BAFTA's, interviewing the likes of Bradley Cooper and George Clooney.

Em's Time Management Techniques

"I found this (time management) really difficult. For me, something had to give, so I wouldn't go on as many nights out as other students and would instead tap away at my laptop. I think working out and eating well is key. If your body is well nourished and you take an hour out a day to clear your mind and work out, even if you just go for some fresh air, you feel refreshed upon returning to your desk. Having a clean workspace really helps me too. I love making lists and find lists help me visualise my workload, as does the calendar function on my laptop. It means I can really organise myself and manage my time well."

You Never Know What A Hobby Could Turn Into

"My blog actually started as an accidental hobby that I slipped into. I rang the admissions tutor at my university and asked how to get onto the course; he told me to start a blog. I wrote about everything and anything, I shared my personal passions and personal ramblings and eventually, a lovely, loyal audience followed the journey with me."

Em's Creative Process

"I write each post differently. I have lists of ideas, for example, top of the list right now is that I want to write a post about body confidence…On days when I have writer's block, I will tweet my followers and ask if there are any topics they'd like me to cover, discussing with them always fills me with ideas. Sometimes, I will go through my most used beauty products for example and photograph them as the basis for a blog post. Travel is always great because a photo tells a thousand words. Other days, something may have happened on that day, and it will spark a personal blog post – it really depends on the day and on the topic."

What would be the one piece of advice you would give your younger self on your first day at university?

"Make more time for social activities. I spent so much time working on my blog that I didn't really join societies or get stuck into any friendship groups. I do feel like I could have left university with more friends, but I was just so busy running businesses that I honestly put my social life on pause."

What's the best book you have ever read?

"I absolutely love *The Great Gatsby* by F. Scott Fitzgerald. I'm a hopeless romantic, and there are so many hidden messages. I love it because the moral of the story is that money doesn't buy you happiness."

Getting Rejected By My Student Newspaper And Then Going On To Co-Found The Biggest Student News Outlet In The World

–JACK RIVLIN

NAME: Jack Rivlin
UNIVERSITY: University of Cambridge
DEGREE: Social and Political Sciences (BA)

Jack Rivlin *(TW: @jackrivlin, www.thetab.com)* is the co-founder and CEO of the student media outlet The Tab. The company gives a platform to student journalists and often covers issues centred on university and student life. Jack co-founded the company while at Cambridge, and The Tab has subsequently expanded to over 110 universities across the UK, USA and Canada. In 2015, The Tab conducted a $3,000,000 funding raise, and in May the site was ranked second in the 18-24 audience category for most visitors, with an audience totalling over 1,600,000 people.

Put The Reader First

"I believe the main reason The Tab has had success is that it puts the audience first and really cares about what they want to read. That doesn't mean pandering to them or being a populist – just like a business owes it to its customers; a journalist owes it to its readers, to tell the truth that matters to them. I think that was our key innovation at the beginning and I believe that we still maintain it. That's why we take pride in actually caring about how many people read our stories. I do care about traffic, I don't think that it's the be all and end all, but I think it's a good measure to go off."

A New Angle Is The Currency Of Journalism

"If you want to be a good journalist and break big stories, it's about finding something new that no one else has got – that is the currency of journalism. When people say *"how do I get a job at a newspaper?"* the first bit of advice they get given to them is *"go to the news desk of that paper with a story"*… The easiest way to find a story is to look at the news and think *"how can I get a new angle on this?"* – For example, Fabric (London nightclub) is closing – *"how can I get a new perspective on this?" What famous DJ's can I go around to and speak to about its closure?"* That would be an obvious new take on the story."

Seek Out Feedback

"Get out and get as much feedback as possible. I speak to a lot of people who start student-facing businesses, and sometimes they think that their idea is something that looks cool to them, but nobody else actually cares about it. It's pretty easy to get real world feedback on your idea – make a minimum viable product of whatever you do. For example, if it was a night club event – run a small one, see how many people want to go and get honest feedback from other people on how well it's going. You have to get out to your customers as early as possible and get feedback from them."

Did you ever face any problems getting people to take you seriously because of your age?

"We live in a weird world now where twenty-year-old university students are massively respected because of Mark Zuckerberg and co. That being said, not being taken seriously is not necessarily a bad thing, it's actually also quite nice to not be taken too seriously when you are young because you can be under the radar and get away with stuff. Respect and attention are something that has to be earned, and that's not a bad thing. It's helpful to be able to grow your business with nobody watching you make mistakes, but I think it's also a discipline to find out how to get people's attention and work hard for it."

Jack's Morning Habit

"Every morning I write down three things that I really don't want to do that day, and I make sure I do them. I really recommend it for getting things done."

What's the funniest moment of your time at university?

"It comes from when we were doing the Tab at Cambridge. We had a lead on a story from someone that there were holes in the condoms in the student's union condom machine. Which if true, would be a really good story – so I went to investigate. Not only would we do that story, but we would also prove how easy it is to break into the university condom supply cupboard and puncture holes into them. (I am sure in hindsight it was the manufacturers' fault, but we were convinced there was some conspiracy going on!) So I snuck my way into their condom cupboard with a camera. I then pushed a safety pin through a condom and took a picture of it with the flash on. The lady in the office next door obviously heard the camera noise and opened the door to see what I was doing… She caught me with a condom in my hand while pushing a safety pin through it! She was so baffled by it I was able to get away – If I caught someone doing that I would have called the police."

SOURCES

Chapter 1 – Goodbye Procrastination; Hello Productivity

1. May-Lyn.N Steets, Robert E.Wickham, Seeing Everyone Else's Highlight Reels: How Facebook Usage Is Linked To Depressive Symptoms, Journal of Social & Clinical Psychology

Chapter 3 – The Student Chef's Cheat Sheet

2. *www.lovefoodhatewaste.com*

Chapter 4 – Staying Out Of Your Overdraft

3. Priya Raghubir, Joydeep Srivastava, Monopoly Money: The Effect of Payment Coupling and Form on Spending Behaviour, Journal of Experimental Psychology

4. Harvard Business Review, Brands Versus Private Labels: Fighting to win

5. Thompson, People Buy More Stuff When They Crave Food, The New Scientist

Chapter 5 – Mo Money, Less Problems

6. James Altucher, Become An Idea Machine: Because Ideas Are The Currency Of The 21st Century

Chapter 6 – Be The 1% Of The Graduate Job Market

7. Totaljobs, 40% of graduates still out of work six months on

8. Ramit Sethi, 'Why my resume got me a job offer at Google'

9. British Council, Languages For The Future: Which languages the UK needs most and why

10. Frontiers in Psychiatry, Effects of Exercise and Physical Activity on Anxiety

Chapter 7 – The Uni Student Health & Fitness Guide

11. BMC Obesity, A meta-analysis of weight gain in first year university students: is freshman 15 a myth?

12. Hungry House, 'Students spend £925 a year on takeaways'

13. Nature Communications, Agrp neuron activity is required for alcohol-induced overeating

14. Dr. Rhonda Patrick, The 'Vitamin D Sweet Spot' And It's Relationship To Aging

15. Dr Rhonda Patrick, Three Main Causes of Megnesium Deficiency

16. Dermatology Research and Practice, Zinc Therapy in Dermatology: A Review

17. Ohio State University for Clinical and Translational Science, Omega-3 Supplementation Lowers Inflammation and Anxiety in Medical Students: A Randomized and Controlled Trlal

18. Alternative Med Rev, 5-Hydroxytryptophan: a clinically-effective serotonin precursor

19. Nikolaou, *Calorie labeling effective in reducing weight gain by 50%*, University of Glasgow, 2nd Annual Obesity Journal Symposium

Chapter 8 – Looking After Your Mind

20. Goldin & Gross, Effects of Mindfulness Based Stress Reduction on Emotional Regulation in Social Anxiety Disorder'

21. Carmody, Mindfulness Practice Leads To Increases in Regional Brain Gray Matter Density

22. Deconstructing the Emotion Regulatory Properties of Mindfulness: An Electrophysiological Investigation

23. Front Psychol, Mindfulness Training Improves Attentional Task Performance In Incarcerated Youth

24. Emmons, Counting Blessing Versus Burdens: An Experimental Investigation of Gratitude and Subjective Well Being In Daily Life

25. Kashdan, Gratitude and Hedonic and Eudaimonic Well-Being in Vietnam War Veterans

26. Fredrickson, What Good Are Positive Emotions In Crises? A Prospective Study Of Resilience and Emotions Following the Terrorist Attacks on the United States on September 11th, 2001

27. Emotion, Warm thanks: gratitude expression facilitates social affiliation in new relationships via perceived warmth.

28. William B Irvine, A Guide to the Good Life: The Ancient Art of Stoic Joy

29. Emotion, Walking facilitates positive affect (even when expecting the opposite)

30. Journal of Experimental Psychology, Give Your Ideas Some Legs: The Positive Effect of Walking on Creative Thinking

31. University of Exeter, Short walk cuts chocolate consumption in half

32. Kahneman, Thinking, Fast and Slow

33. Psychological Momentum: Why Success Breeds Success Seppo E. Iso-Ahola and Charles O. Dotson (2014) University of Maryland

Chapter 9 – Hack Your Hangover

34. Wiese, The Alcohol Hangover

35. Rohsenow, Intoxication with Bourbon Versus Vodka: Effects on Hangover, Sleep and Next-Day Neurocognitive Performance in Young Adults

36. Chapman, Experimental Induction of Hangover

37. University of Marlyland Medical Centre, *Milk Thistle*

38. Linednborg, Reducing Carcinogenic Acetaldehyde Exposure in the Achlorhydric Stomach with Cysteine

39. Scrivens, Rebounding: Good for the Lymph System

Chapter 10 – Becoming A Social Buttefly

40. Gilovich, Spotlight Effect In Social Judgment: An Egocentric Bias In Estimates of the Salience of One's Own Actions and Appearance

41. Gordon PHD, 'Have You Fallen Prey To The "Spotlight Effect"

42. Northern Illnois University, Shyness Mindset: Applying mindset theory to the domain of inhibited social behaviour

43. Tracy, The expression of pride and shame: Evidence for biologically innate nonverbal displays

44. TED, Your body language may shape who you are, Amy Cuddy

45. TEDx, How to become more confident – lay down on the street for 30sec

46. Scholey, Chewing gum alleviates negative mood and reduces cortisol during acute laboratory psychological stress

47. eHarmony, Over 50% of couples will meet online by 2031

48. Skout, When Online Dating Goes Mobile

49. Cornell University Library, A First Look at User Activity on Tinder

50. Yulya Besplemenova, What Statistics Tells About Tinder (and HOW TO GET MORE MATCHES)

51. Journal of Fashion Marketing and Management: An International Journal, the influence of clothing on first impressions: Rapid and minor responses to minor changes in male attire

52. Journal of Experimental Psychology

53. OkCupid, The 4 Big Myths Of Profile Pictures

54. Université de Bretagne-Sud, Domestic Dogs as Facilitators in Social Interaction: An Evalutation of Helping and Courtship Behaviours

55. Business Insider, The best body language to use in your online-dating profile, according to science

56. Psychology of Music, Men's music ability and attractiveness to women in a real-life courtship context

57. How to Persuade Others with the Right Questions: Jedi Mind Tricks from Daniel H Pink

Chapter 11 – The Night Out

58. Internaitonal Journal Of Cosmetic Science, Manipulation of body odour alters men's self-confidence and judgements of their visual attractiveness by women

59. The Date Report, 'Being Confident Will Get You More Dates Than Being Attractive', Says Science

ACKNOWLEDGEMENTS

First, I must thank all the Insightees who agreed to be in this book and share their wisdom. It was an absolute pleasure. I am looking forward to what you will all go on to accomplish, on top of your already incredible achievements.

This book would be nothing without David Jacob. Thanks for being the Yoda to my Luke Skywalker.

To Naikee Kohli and Phil Daneshyar, this was just an idea until I posted it in in our Whatsapp group chat. Regardless of the highs and lows, you boys are always there. Let the Whatsapp group continue to be a birthplace for action!

To Charlotte Owens, who was the first person that saw the horrendous first few drafts and helped get the wheels moving on the project, you are a star. Since I heard that beautiful Liverpudlian accent on my first day at university, I knew we would have a great time together. The cooking lessons are forever appreciated.

Reece Best, our regular coffees at Starbucks, workouts at JD fitness and pints at the Arms were always a welcome distraction. I'll see you at a Techno rave soon I'm sure.

To Joe Henshaw, thanks for the amazing cover and putting up with the constant changes. The Office and Alan Partridge references made it much easier though. It was textbook, now go and get the guitar!

Refining this book was an absolute nightmare. It took one year longer than expected to write this book. The torturous process was made easier by the likes of Charlie Wodehouse, Sophia Hill and Eddie Royle who helped sieve out the gold.

This book is dedicated to every person I met at university. My heart will always be at Derwent College. Keep ignoring those nasty chants from other jealous colleges.

Particular mentions go to Tom Gill, Guy Giles and Previn Desai for always making me tear up with laughter. Hopefully one day we will all be reunited in Mambo Lounge (well anything but Flares!)

Thanks to my other legendary housemates Charlie McLaughlin, Will Scott and Celia Harker for putting up with me and letting me keep that bedroom. Keep on sheen-ing, caving and loving life respectively!

To Jack Spring, thank you for teaching me that a hangover is a mental construct.

I got a ridiculous amount of support from my student union and the commercial services while at university. Thank you for taking the time to help a young lad who had absolutely no clue what he was doing.

To Muhammad the AA guy who filled up my petrol tank, if you ever get to read this, I owe you one!

If I were to write a list of people who have helped me out in the last twelve months, it would be longer than this book, and I'd still forget a few! That being said, thanks goes to Josh 'Kaboom' Kalms, Jasmine 'Trouble' Trobe, Shez 'Bicep' Mirza, Max 'This Guy' Holland, Tess 'Food' Bannister and Joe 'Date Night' Stone for making my life a lot more enjoyable.

To my younger brother Harry, who has more mental strength in his finger than I have in my entire body – If you keep practising, you may one day beat me at FIFA! To my older brother Peter, thank you for the guitar solos and all the amazing movie recommendations.

Last but not least, my parents, thank you for always instilling confidence and supporting me. I couldn't have asked for a better hand in life. You are the best.

George MacGill

I'll aim to keep this short, as anyone who knows me knows I will ramble on for hours if you let me. Firstly, I must thank George for allowing me to help with this project. From the get-go, I knew it had the potential to be a fantastic book, and I'm so glad I had the opportunity to be a part of something like this. Happy I could help, Charlie Babbitt.

To all the boys I lived with this year, Charlie Winterburn, Leslie Oppon, Lewis Harrison, Dom Hayes and Dom Williams, thank you for putting up with my constant, rambling conversations about nothing but this, I know how taxing that would have been for you!

To Sheni Salami and Craig Jantzen, thank you both for your fantastic recommendations of the best books to read and for being an enormous help with contrasting literature and research, you both had a massive role in my thought process throughout. Ben Mouquet, thank you for patiently listening to my incessant rants about nothing in particular, and being the twin that I never thought I'd want, need or have – you've been an absolute gem.

To Eleanor Steel and Poonam Mistry, thank you both for your enthusiasm, your keen grammatical and literary eyes, and moreover dealing with having me as a friend for longer than I can remember. You're both incredible, and I'm so glad I could come to you both after not speaking for a while and have your unwavering support and help with this.

To Jason Mathew-Mammen and Matthew Abraham, thank you both for offering professional advice that would have cost us a hell of a lot at your usual rates! Jason you're a true role model and someone that truly makes me believe that bonds decide family, not blood. A mention to Tanya Dixon at Gpex who provided fantastic design advice early on as a favour, it was greatly appreciated!

Lynn Sheppard, thank you for taking the time to hear me out when I randomly walked into your office and elevator pitched you, your support through this has been greatly appreciated!

Tayte Nickols, for being an audio and tech wizard and sorting us out with the audiobook, you're the real OG. Thank you to everyone else who has added their unique thoughts and comments throughout, you have all been incredibly helpful, and I couldn't have asked for a better group of people around me during what was an extremely stressful time. Bryony Collins, for being so wonderfully critical and offering corrections, ideas and completely different perspectives at every point, and being a welcome person to bounce ideas off. You were honestly invaluable as neither George or I had thought of the points you raised.

Finally, thanks to my parents, whose complete confidence, support and love throughout were the only things that kept me functional during all the stressful days and all-nighters. I couldn't have done it without you.

David Jacob

Printed in Poland
by Amazon Fulfillment
Poland Sp. z o.o., Wrocław